BLOOD SIMPLE

BLOOD SIMPLE

An Original Screenplay by

JOEL COEN
and
ETHAN COEN

ST. MARTIN'S PRESS NEW YORK

Design by Judith Stagnitto

Front cover photo and photos in text by Blaine Pennington

Library of Congress Cataloging-in-Publication Data

Coen, Joel.
  Blood simple / Joel and Ethan Coen.
    p. cm. — (St. Martin's original screenplay series)
  Screenplay for the motion picture Blood simple.
  ISBN 0-312-02168-2
  I. Coen, Ethan. II. Blood simple (Motion picture) III. Title.
  IV. Series.
  PN1997.B673 1988
  791.43'72—dc19   88–12018
                                    CIP

10 9 8 7 6 5 4

Preface

"What was your shooting ratio?"

It is a question often asked at festival and college screenings of our movies. The question means, how did the total footage shot compare to the total footage of the completed picture? For some reason the question fascinates people the world over, while other pointlessly precise questions are never asked. No one asks about our teamster ratio, for instance, which compares the total number of teamsters employed on the picture to the number of teamsters who worked. Nor does anyone ask about our paper ratio, which compares the total number of pages of notes and drafts to the hundred or so pages of finished screenplay manuscript. But the fact that no one is interested enough to ask doesn't preclude our answering, and we have chosen this last question as our theme.

A reader of the finished script to which these remarks serve as prolegomenon might well wonder, if this is the stuff they thought was good enough to shoot, what could they possibly have thrown out? Fair question, and we will shortly provide a sample. First, however, we would like to point out that, excepting present remarks, virtually all written material underwent a process of revision and redrafting. This is a time-honored tradition and among professional writers it carries no stigma and is not considered "cheating." Rarely is the reading public given the opportunity to inspect an author's mucilaginous crude before it is refined and transmuted into what Heinrich Heine once called "gaz." Few realize, for instance, that the first draft of Herman Melville's grand meditation on the vasty deep began, "Just call me Ishmael." In revision, fortunately, the bearded bard of the bounding main deleted his chef d'oeuvre's first word; we may be grateful also that Pittsfield's Homer expanded the name of his eponymous behemoth from the first draft's folksy but retentive "Dick."

How fortunate that, in sculpting one of his classic sonnets, Shakespeare applied so ruthless a chisel to the first draft:

> When to the sessions of sweet silent thought
> We summon up remembrance of things from a long time
>   ago . . .

In the first draft of *Macbeth*, the Bard of Avon had his gloomy Gael reflect on life:

> It is a tale told by an idiot
> Full of sound and fury
> And all manner of things.

Sensing room for improvement, the author concocted a new epiphany for his dyspeptic highlander:

> It is a tale told by an idiot
> Full of sound and fury
> Nor meaneth it a thing.

In the third draft, the poet put these words into the mouth of his henpecked Scot:

It is a tale told by an egret
Full of sound and fury
Signifying nothing.

Well, one step forward, one step back.

And so it was with *Blood Simple*. For instance, in an early draft of the script, Ray, the befuddled bartender who for want of a more compelling character served as our story's hero, fled the scene of the tale's protracted central murder and checked into a motel outside of San Antonio:

MOTEL LOBBY DAY

DUSTY RHODES, *a lean man with a weathered face and large Adam's apple, stands behind the Formica check-in counter.* KYLE, *a heavyset man of thirty wearing a feed cap, sits in the lobby's one piece of furniture, a beat-up leatherette sofa. He sips from a can of soda.*

RAY, *begrimed and haggard, enters out of the glare of the noonday sun.*

RHODES: Hey there, stranger! What can I do you for?

RAY: I need a room.

Calling out from the divan:

KYLE: He needs a room, Dusty.

RHODES: I reckon I can hear him . . .

. . . (*to* RAY) Room rate's eight sixty-six a day plus sales tax, plus extra for the TV option.

RAY: How much extra?

KYLE (*calling out*):   He wants the TV option, Dusty.

RHODES: I reckon I can hear him. TV option, that's a dollar twenty, makes nine eighty-six plus tax.

KYLE (*calling out*):   Tell him the channels, Dusty.

RHODES: Channels, we got two and six. Two don't come in so hot.

RAY: Just a room then.

KYLE (*calling out*):   He don't want the option, Dusty.

RHODES: I reckon I heard the man.

RAY (*after shooting* KYLE *an irritated glance*):   Does he work here?

KYLE (*calling out*):   Sure don't.

RHODES: See, Wednesday's the special on RC Cola. I don't know if I explained about the TV option. If there's a TV in the room, you got to pay the option.

KYLE (*calling out*):   And how many rooms got TV, Dusty?

RHODES: Ever durned one.

RAY (*gamely*):   Okay, I'll take the TV option.

RHODES: Well see the thing about that is, we're booked.

Looking at this scene now, years later, it strikes us that revising it out of existence, as we did, constituted too much rewriting. Indeed, the more prosaic scene we replaced it with, involving Ray stopped at a traffic light, can be found in the finished script but not in the finished movie. It was shot but then deleted in order to more quickly get to the carnage, which was the picture's raison d'être.

In fact—for those of you who have seen the movie—in an early draft of the climactic scene the heroine, after impaling the private detective's hand on the window sill, saws off his captive fingers and pops them through the holes that he has shot into the wall that separates them. An even earlier draft had her first pull the nails off the disembodied fingers with a grimping hook, but we were advised that this might frighten small children.

So finally, by trimming the script instead of the digits of our hapless private snoop, we arrived at the paradigm of restraint that is now the climax of the movie. "Sellout!" some people will say. But one must remember that Art and Commerce are uneasy bedfellows 'neath picturedom's sheets, nor may they even shake hands without spraining something.

But we mentioned earlier that we were "advised" in this matter, which brings us to another aspect of the writing process.

Young writers just starting out and eager to make good should know that the world teems with critics—ugly, bitter people, fat and acned for the most part, often afflicted with gout, dropsy, and diseases of the inner ear. Always they know better; always they recognize just exactly what is missing; always, always they can point the way to a finer choice.

That is why, on occasion, we search them out. But beware: Though the critic can tell you how to improve, he will never tell you what is equally important, when to stop improving. The critic is a lonely man, and a crafty one.

He knows that if he tells you your work is finished,

then you will also be finished listening to him; and so he indefatigably navigates, while you long for a sign that your voyage is over—as does, no doubt, the traveler through these remarks. Dizzied and dazed by a lack of organization, he himself back now, Magellanlike, at the point of origin. What was our paper ratio? How much rewriting is enough? How much is too much? When do you quit?

Even did he wish to, the critic couldn't answer, for he doesn't know. He might believe that you quit revising a manuscript when it is "right." He might also believe that a bell sounds on the floor of the stock exchange when the Dow has reached its high for the day. Neither will the professional writer tell you the rule for when to stop writing, because he is insecure, fearful of giving up trade secrets and losing his competitive edge. We'll tell you, because we're in the movie business and so our careers depend upon public caprice rather than on the play of competitive market forces. The rule is, you quit rewriting when your manuscript starts to bore you. Only the amateur, who has boundless energy and who lacks the imagination to quit, ever works beyond that point.

Consult, then, your heart. Once your work feels stale and tiresome you should present it to the public. Anyway, that's what we do.

J.C. and E.C.
New York
August 1988

Credits

The Players

Ray	John Getz
Abby	Frances McDormand
Julian Marty	Dan Hedaya
Private Detective	M. Emmet Walsh
Meurice	Samm-Art Williams
Debra	Deborah Neumann
Landlady	Raquel Gavia
Man from Lubbock	Van Brooks
Mr. Garcia	Señor Marco
Old Cracker	William Creamer
Strip Bar Exhorter	Loren Bivens
Strip Bar Senator	Bob McAdams
Stripper	Shannon Sedwick
Girl on Overlook	Nancy Finger
Radio Evangelist	Rev. William Preston Robertson

Directed by	Joel Coen
Produced by	Ethan Coen
Written by	Joel Coen and Ethan Coen
Executive Producer	Daniel F. Bacaner
Associate Producer	Mark Silverman
Director of Photography	Barry Sonnenfeld
Production Designer	Jane Musky
Music by	Carter Burwell
Edited by	Roderick Jaynes and Don Wiegmann
First Assistant Director	Deborah Reinisch

Casting	Julie Hughes and Barry Moss
Special Effects Coordinator	Loren Bivens
Location Manager and Austin Casting	Edith M. Clark
Second Assistant Director	Steve Love
Third Assistant Director	Shannon Wood
Location Coordinator	Don Hartack
Production Office Coordinator	Alma Kuttruff
Assistant to Production Designer	Steve Roll
Property Master	Shirley Belwood
Property Assistant	Marcos E. Gonzalez
Focus Puller	David Frederick
Clapper/Loader	Don Kirk
Sound Mixer	Lee Orloff
Boom	Peter F. Kurland
Gaffer	Joey Forsyte
Second Electric	Julie Gant
Electricians	Don Wiegmann
	John Shaw
Key Grip	Tom Prophet, Jr.
Best Boy	Richard Creasy
Third Grip	Angelo Suasnovar
Make-Up	Jean Ann Black
Wardrobe Designers	Sara Medina-Pape
	Chelle Coleman
Script Supervisor	Andreas Laven
Location Editor	Peggy Connolly
Special Effects Make-Up and Prosthetics	Paul R. Smith
Special Effects Mechanical	Michael K. O'Sullivan
Set Dresser	Nancy Griffith
Art Department Assistants	Bob Sturtevant
	Jeff Adams
	Michael Peal
	Kathy Baker
	Dave Pearce
Special Graphics	Beth Parry
Photo Retoucher	David Wander
Special Stills	Blaine Pennington
Editorial Consultant	Edna Ruth Paul
Sound Editors	Skip Lievsay
	Michael R. Miller

Special Sound Effects	Fred Szymanski
	Jun Mizumachi
Music Coordinator and Production	Murri Barber
Re-recording Mixer	Mel Zelniker
Location Auditor	H. Harris Willcockson
Dog Trainer	Marty Mahoney
Dialect Coach	Lizanne Brazell
Casting Associates	Peter Golden
	Phil DiMaggio
Negative Cutter	Victor Concepcion
Title Design	Dan Perri
Production Assistants	Van Brooks
	Ingrid Weigand
	David McGill
	Melanie Hecht
	Webster Lewin
	Darrell Kreitz
	Adam Smith
	John Woodward
	Richard Woolsey
	Shawn Malone
	Tom Martin
Color by	DuArt
Post-Production Services by	The Spera Corporation and
	Sound One Corporation
Optical Effects by	The Optical House, New York
Special Thanks to	Hilary Ney
	Earl Miller
	Ivan Bigley
	Renaissance Pictures
	Ron Seres
	George Majesski
	C. Wilson Interiors
	Abel Stationers
	Computerland of Austin
	Texas Film Commission

Shot on Location in Austin and Hutto, Texas

BLOOD
SIMPLE

LANDSCAPES

An opening voice-over plays against dissolving Texas landscapes—broad, bare, and lifeless.

VOICE-OVER: The world is full of complainers. But the fact is, nothing comes with a guarantee. I don't care if you're the Pope of Rome, President of the United States, or even Man of the Year—something can always go wrong. And go ahead, complain, tell your problems to your neighbor, ask for help—watch him fly.

Now in Russia, they got it mapped out so that everyone pulls for everyone else—that's the theory, anyway. But what I know about is Texas . . .

CUT TO:

ROAD NIGHT

We are rushing down a rain-swept country road, listening to the rhythmic swish of tires on wet asphalt.

And down here . . . you're on your own.

INT CAR NIGHT

We are looking at the backs of two people in the front seat—a man, driving, and a woman next to him.

Their conversation will be punctuated by the occasional glare of oncoming headlights and the roar of the car rushing by.
The windshield wipers wave a soporific beat. The conversation is halting, awkward.

WOMAN: . . . He gave me a little pearl-handled .38 for our first anniversary.

MAN: Uh-huh.

WOMAN: . . . Figured I'd better leave before I used it on him. I don't know how you can stand him.

MAN: Well, I'm only an employee, I ain't married to him.

WOMAN: Yeah . . .

Pause, as an oncoming car passes. Finally:

. . . I don't know. Sometimes I think there's something wrong with him. Like maybe he's sick? Mentally? . . . Or is it maybe me, do you think?

MAN: Listen, I ain't a marriage counselor. I don't know what goes on, I don't wanna know . . . But I like you. I always liked you . . .

Another car passes.

. . . What're you gonna do in Houston?

WOMAN: I'll figure something out . . . How come you offered to drive me in this mess?

MAN: I told you. I like you.

WOMAN: See, I never knew that.

MAN: Well now you do.

WOMAN: . . . Hell.

Another pause, another car.
Suddenly:

WOMAN: Stop the car, Ray!

CLOSE SHOT BRAKE

Stamped on.

EXT CAR

Low three-quarters on the car as it squeals to a halt.
A car that has been following screeches to a halt just behind
it.
Both cars sit.
Rain patters.

INT FIRST CAR

Close on the man, from behind.
He looks at the woman.

MAN: . . . Abby?

She doesn't answer. He turns to look back and we see his face,
for the first time, in the headlights of the car behind.

HIS POV

The car behind them waiting, patiently. Rain drifts down
past its headlights.

Finally it pulls out and passes them slowly, their headlights showing it to be a battered green Volkswagen. First the car itself, then its red taillights, disappear into the rain.

BACK TO THE MAN

Cutting between him and the woman, each from behind.

MAN: . . . You know that car?

WOMAN: No.

MAN: What's the matter?

WOMAN: I don't know . . . I just think maybe I'm making a mistake . . .

She looks at the man.

. . . What was that back there?

MAN: Back where.

WOMAN: Sign.

MAN: I don't know. Motel . . . Abby—

WOMAN: Ray. Did you mean that, what you said before, or were you just being a gentleman?

MAN: Abby, I like you, but it's no point starting anything now.

WOMAN: Yeah.

MAN: I mean, I ain't a marriage counselor—

WOMAN: Yeah.

The man is uncomfortable.

MAN: . . . What do you want to do?

The woman is uncomfortable. After a long pause:

WOMAN: . . . What do *you* want to do?

MOTEL ROOM

Pulling back from RAY *and* ABBY *in bed, making love.*
The only light is from cars passing along the highway
outside. Each sweeping light-by ends in black.
The pullback ends in a wide shot of the motel room. The
black following the last car-by lingers.
A telephone rings.

SAME WIDE SHOT   MORNING

RAY *and* ABBY *are asleep. On a nightstand next to the bed,*
the telephone is ringing.
RAY *stirs, reaches for the phone.*

RAY: . . . Hello.

VOICE: Having a good time?

RAY: . . . What? Who is this?

VOICE: I don't know, who's this?

A silence at both ends.

. . . You still there?

RAY: Yeah, I'm still here.

RAY *listens to another silence. It ends with a disconnect.*
ABBY *is stirring as* RAY *gets out of bed.*

ABBY: . . . Ray?

RAY: Yeah.

ABBY: What was that?

RAY: Your husband.

BAR BACK OFFICE   NIGHT

*We are tracking past a man seated behind a wooden desk,
towards an 8 × 10 black-and-white photograph that has just
been slapped down on the desktop.*
   The picture is of ABBY *and* RAY *in bed together in the motel
room.*

VOICE: I know a place you can get that framed.

*The voice is familiar as that of the narrator whose musings on
life in Texas and the Soviet Union opened the movie.*
   We cut to him.
   He is settling himself into a chair facing the desk. He is
LOREN VISSER, *a large unshaven man in a misshapen yellow
leisure suit.*
   He smiles at the man behind the desk.

JULIAN MARTY

*sits staring down at the photograph. Behind him a window
opens on the bar proper. Country-western music filters in
from the bar.*
   MARTY *is not pleased.*

MARTY: What did you take these for?

VISSER: What do you mean . . .

Dan Hedaya (Marty)

He removes a pouch of tobacco from his breast pocket and nonchalantly starts rolling a cigarette.

. . . Just doin' my job.

MARTY: You called me, I knew they were there, so what do I need these for?

VISSER: Well, I don't know . . . Call it a fringe benefit.

MARTY: How long did you watch her?

VISSER: Most of the night . . .

*He lights his cigarette, then slaps his lighter onto the desktop.
    It is silver, engraved on the top with a lariat spelling out "Loren" in script, and on the side with a declaration that he is "Elks Man of the Year."*

. . . They'd just rest a few minutes and then get started again. Quite something.

MARTY stares down at the photograph.

MARTY: You know in Greece they cut off the head of the messenger who brought bad news.

A smoke ring floats into frame from offscreen.

VISSER: Now that don't make much sense.

MARTY: No. It just made them feel better.

MARTY rises and goes to a safe behind his desk.
VISSER laughs as he watches MARTY.

VISSER: Well first off, Julian, I don't know what the story is in Greece but in this state we got very definite laws about that . . .

MARTY, hunched over the standing safe behind his desk, tosses in the photograph and takes out a pay envelope.

. . . Second place I ain't a messenger, I'm a private investigator. And third place—and most important—it ain't such bad news. I mean you thought he was a colored (*he laughs*) . . . You're always assumin' the worst . . .

VISSER blows another smoke ring, pushes a fat finger through the middle of it, and beams at MARTY.

. . . Anything else?

MARTY: Yeah, don't come by here any more. If I need you again I know which rock to turn over.

MARTY *scales the pay envelope across the desk. It hits* VISSER *in the chest and bounces to the floor.*
VISSER *looks stonily down at the envelope; no expression for a beat. Then he roars with laughter.*

VISSER: That's good . . . "which rock to turn over"
. . . that's very good . . .

Sighing, he leans forward to pick up the envelope. He rises, straightens his cowboy hat, and walks over to a screen door letting out on the bar's back parking lot.

VISSER: Well, gimme a call whenever you wanna cut off my head . . .

He pauses at the door, cocks his head, then turns back to the desk and picks up his cigarette lighter. Returning to the door:

. . . I can crawl around without it.

The door slams shut behind him.
MARTY *scowls at the back door. After a moment he rises and crosses the office to the window looking out on the bar.*
Over MARTY'S *shoulder we see the long bar leading up to the window in perpendicular. The camera is tracking forward, past* MARTY, *to frame on the window.*
A black man is just now vaulting the near end of the bar, over onto the customer side.

MATCH CUT TO:
MARTY'S BAR
REVERSE ANGLE   VAULTING MAN

Tracking back with him as he lands on the customer side and heads across the bar. This shot, from the other side of the back-office window, reveals the window to be a one-way glass mirrored on this side.
MEURICE, *the black bartender, is muscular, about 200*

*pounds, dressed in white pants and a sleeveless T-shirt. He is
making his way through the crowd toward the jukebox.
Another man stands in front of it examining the selections.
He deposits a quarter.*

MEURICE: Hold it, hold it. What's tonight?

MAN: What?

MEURICE: What night is it?

MAN (*studying* MEURICE):   . . . Friday?

MEURICE: Right. Friday night is Yankee night. Where're
you from?

MAN: Lubbock?

*MEURICE shakes his head and punches the selector buttons on
the jukebox.*

MEURICE: Right. I'm from Detroit (*turning to leave*). It's
a big city up north with tall buildings.

*A Motown song drops. We track behind MEURICE as he
makes his way back toward the bar. When he reaches it, he
claps a couple of people on the shoulder, who make way for
him. He vaults back over the top, walks down the bar, and
stops in front of an attractive white woman sitting on a bar
stool and sipping a brandy.*

MEURICE: Where was I?

WOMAN: You were telling me about the Ring of Fire.

MEURICE: Yeah, well, I may be getting in over my head
here, I mean you're the geologist, but my theory for what

it's worth, you got all these volcanoes and each time each one pops it's the equivalent of what, twenty, thirty megatons of TNT? enough to light Vegas for how long? how many years? Course, I'm no mathematician but—

MARTY: Meurice.

MARTY is approaching from the direction of the office.

MEURICE: Yeah, I know. Pour 'em short.

MARTY: Has Ray come in yet?

MEURICE: No, he's off tonight. Where was he last night?

MARTY (*glaring*): How would I know?

MEURICE: I don't know, didn't he call?

MARTY loses his glare and his gaze drifts over to the woman. After an awkward pause, MEURICE clears his throat.

. . . Marty, I'd like you to meet an old friend of mine, Debra. Debra, this is Julian Marty, the dude I'm always talking about.

She is unselfconsciously returning MARTY's stare.

MARTY: If he does come in I'm not here . . . What were you drinking, Debra?

DEBRA: Remy.

MARTY: You've got a very sophisticated palate.

DEBRA: Thanks.

MARTY: Give Debra here another drink, and give me
the usual.

MEURICE walks down the bar.

DEBRA: . . . What's a palate?

MARTY studies her for a beat, she studies him, he smiles.

MARTY: Listen, I got tickets for the Oilers and the Rams
next week in the Astrodome. Ever sat on the fifty yard
line?

DEBRA: I don't follow baseball.

MARTY laughs.

MARTY: You won't have to. I'll explain what a palate is.

DEBRA: You won't have to. I just wanted to see if you
knew.

*MARTY smiles bleakly. DEBRA drains her glass as MEURICE
returns. He sets another Cognac in front of DEBRA, and a
glass of milk in front of Marty.*

MARTY: What's this?

MEURICE: You said the usual—

MARTY: Red Label.

MEURICE (*picking up the milk*):   Right. Sorry.

MARTY: Pour that back.

MEURICE: What.

MARTY: Don't throw that out.

MEURICE: Right.

He wanders on down the bar; MARTY's *attention returns to the woman.*

MARTY: So how long have you known Meurice?

DEBRA: About ten years.

MARTY's *attention is caught by something down the bar. He half-rises from his stool.*

MARTY: What—Waitaminute—What . . .

HIS POV

MEURICE *is pouring the milk down the sink. He looks innocently up.*

MEURICE: What.

BACK TO MARTY

Angry but not knowing what to say. He glances around the bar, sinks slowly back onto his stool.

MARTY: Deuce in the corner needs help.

MEURICE: Right.

MARTY *sits staring across the bar for a moment, nods a couple of times at nothing in particular, then looks back at the woman.*

MARTY: . . . So what're you doing tonight?

DEBRA: Going out with Meurice.

MARTY *tosses a beer nut into his mouth.*

MARTY: Tell him you have a headache.

DEBRA *gives him a level stare.*

DEBRA: It'll pass.

MARTY: We don't seem to be communicating—

DEBRA: You want to hustle me. I don't want to be hustled. It's as simple as that. Now that I've communicated, why don't you leave?

MARTY: I own the place.

DEBRA: Christ, I'm getting bored.

MARTY: I'm not surprised, the company you've been keeping the last ten years.

They both fall silent as MEURICE *enters frame. He takes a bottle from the bar and pours himself a drink.*

MARTY: What's this?

MEURICE: What.

MARTY (*pointing at* MEURICE's *drink*):   This.

MEURICE: Jack Daniels. Don't worry, I'm paying for it.

MARTY: That's not the point.

MEURICE: What's the point?

MARTY: The point is we don't serve niggers here.

MEURICE: Where? (*He looks over his shoulder; up and down the bar*) . . . I'm very careful about that.

MARTY tosses back MEURICE's drink, then turns to DEBRA, smiling.

MARTY: He thinks I'm kidding. Everybody thinks I'm kidding; (*as he turns to leave*) if Ray comes in I'm not home.

DEBRA watches him go, then turns back to MEURICE.

DEBRA: Nice guy.

MEURICE: Not really. What'd you say your last name was?

MARTY'S HOUSE   TRACKING DOWN HALLWAY

We are following a large German shepherd as it pads down the hall toward a warmly lit room at its end. We hear only the sound of the dog's paws on the hardwood floor, and the faint clicking of billiard balls.

BILLIARD ROOM

It is a paneled, carpeted room with black leather furniture and a nine-foot billiard table. Various stuffed animal trophies are scattered around the room, including a moose head mounted on one wall. RAY stands alone in the foreground, shooting pool, an unlit cigarette in his mouth. The room is very quiet.

In the background the German shepherd enters from the hallway, sits down in a corner, and benignly watches RAY.

UPSTAIRS BEDROOM

It is expensively appointed; a brightly lit woman's bedroom. ABBY is opening a hinged drawer in a white antique bureau. She pulls out a leather handbag, gropes nervously through its contents, then puts it aside.

She crosses the room to a vanity table, takes a purse from underneath, and spills its contents out on top of the table.

BILLIARD ROOM

RAY *pockets a couple of balls, looks over at the dog, then up at the wall at the far end of the room.*

RAY'S POV

Hanging on the wall are a couple of framed photographs of MARTY *and* ABBY, *taken a long time ago.*

BACK TO RAY

Staring at the pictures. He looks back down at the pool table.

UPSTAIRS BEDROOM

ABBY *is sitting on a large double bed. She puts aside another purse, rises and crosses the room hurriedly, and pushes back the sliding doors of a long wardrobe closet. The upper shelf is lined with handbags—fifteen or twenty of them. She grabs the first one, looks in, tosses it aside; grabs the second, looks—and stops.*

HER POV

Inside the purse, a small pearl-handled gun.

BILLIARD ROOM

RAY *is now standing in front of the pictures on the wall, looking from one to the next.*

RAY'S POV

A picture of ABBY *and* MARTY *standing together on a Gulf beach.* MARTY *is wearing a long velour beach robe,* ABBY *is in a swimming suit.* RAY's *hand enters frame. He traces a finger down her leg.*

CLOSE SHOT   RAY

His head cocked to the side. After a moment his eyes shift.

EXTREME CLOSE SHOT   PHOTO DETAIL

Of MARTY'S *face. He is staring into the camera, at whoever took the picture. His head is thrown back slightly; he is laughing.*

From offscreen in the quiet room we hear a static hum and then ABBY'S *voice over an intercom.*

ABBY'S VOICE: Ray. . .?

BACK TO RAY

He turns from the photograph and walks to an intercom speaker next to the mounted moose's head. He presses the speaker button.

RAY: Yeah . . .

He idly takes his unlit cigarette and sticks it in the moose's mouth.

. . . You get what you wanted?

ABBY'S VOICE: Yeah. Let's get out of here.

MARTY'S FRONT FOYER

We are looking across a dark, high-ceilinged foyer toward the front door. RAY *leans against the doorjamb, in silhouette in the open doorway. He is facing a curved staircase that descends into the foyer.* ABBY *appears at the second-floor landing and starts down the stairs.*

RAY: Why d'you wanna leave all this?

ABBY: You kidding? I don't wanna leave all this, I just wanna leave Marty . . .

As she reaches the bottom of the stairs:

. . . Drive me to a motel?

RAY: You can stay at my place, I'll drop you there.

ABBY: Where . . . where you going?

RAY: See a guy.

ABBY (*nervously*): Don't go to the bar, Ray. I know him, that ain't a good idea.

RAY: I just gotta see a guy.

MARTY'S BAR

The crowd has thinned out. MEURICE and DEBRA are in the foreground.
  RAY enters from the street and makes his way over to them.

MEURICE: Howdy stranger.

RAY: Meurice. Sorry I didn't show last night.

MEURICE: Wasn't too busy. You missed a good one, though. This white guy walks in about one o'clock, asks if we have a discount for alcoholics . . .
  I tell him to get lost, but Marty's sitting here listening and I can tell he's thinking that maybe it ain't such a bad idea . . .

He pours DEBRA another drink and starts to set one up for RAY.

. . . Ray, this is Debra. She's a geologist. That's the theory of rocks.

RAY *nods at* DEBRA.

RAY: Is Marty here?

MEURICE: Not here tonight. Wasn't here last night. He's especially not back in his office.

RAY (*leaving*):   Thanks Meurice.

MEURICE: For what?

EXT   BACK OF MARTY'S BAR

MARTY *is sitting on the stoop that descends from his back office to a graveled back parking lot; he is framed in the open doorway of his brightly lit office. He stares fixedly at something offscreen.*

MARTY'S POV

In the middle distance a huge incinerator operates full blast. Orange flames lick out the sides; white smoke billows out the top. Two figures in silhouette are chucking garbage in through a large gate.

BACK TO MARTY

Behind him, in the office, we see the door from the bar open, and RAY *entering.*

RAY: Marty?

MARTY *looks over his shoulder, then back toward the furnace.* RAY *descends the stoop and stands in front of him.*

. . . Well. . . ? What?

MARTY stares past RAY across the parking lot.

MARTY: What "what"?

RAY: Am I fired? You wanna hit me? What?

MARTY: I don't particularly want to talk to you.

RAY: Well . . . if you're not gonna fire me I might as well quit.

MARTY: Fine. Suit yourself (*still staring fixedly at the furnace*) . . . Having a good time?

RAY tenses. There is a pause.

RAY: . . . I don't like this kind of talk.

MARTY still stares at the furnace.

MARTY: Then what'd you come here for?

RAY (*no more conciliation*):   You owe me for two weeks.

MARTY shakes his head.

MARTY: Nope. She's an expensive piece of ass . . .

He finally looks up at RAY.

. . . You get a refund though, if you tell me who else she's been sluicing.

RAY: I want that money. If you wanna tell me something, fine—

MARTY: What're you, a fucking marriage counselor?

RAY breaks into a strained half-smile.
MARTY grins humorlessly back, mimicking RAY's smile.

MARTY: What're you smiling at—I'm a funny guy,
right, I'm an asshole? No no, that's not what's funny.
What's funny is her. What's funny is that I had you two
followed because, if it isn't you, she's been sleeping with
someone else . . .

*He grabs a knee in each hand and leans forward, still looking
at RAY. He is becoming only slightly more animated.*

. . . What's really going to be funny is when she gives
you that innocent look and says, What're you talking
about, Ray, I haven't done anything funny . . .

He leans back again.

. . . But the funniest thing to me right now is that you
think she came back here for you—*that's* what's funny.

*RAY moves forward and MARTY's eyes follow him as he
approaches. MARTY's smile abruptly turns to a look of
apprehension. RAY enters frame and brushes past MARTY as
he walks up the stoop, and crosses the back office toward the
bar.*
MARTY relaxes, and his gaze returns to the furnace.

. . . Come on this property again and I'll be forced to
shoot you . . .

RAY opens the door to the bar and shuts it softly behind him.

. . . Fair notice.

MARTY'S OFFICE   LATER
CLOSE SHOT   CEILING FAN

At the cut the music and all other bar noise drops out. We hear only the rhythmic whir of the fan. We tilt down from the ceiling fan to frame MARTY, *tilted back in his desk chair, staring up at the fan.*

MEURICE (*OS*):   Marty . . .

WIDE SHOT   THE OFFICE

MEURICE *is standing in the door to the bar. Far behind him we can see* DEBRA *waiting in the dimly lit, deserted bar.*

MEURICE: . . . I thought you were dead. Going home?

MARTY: No. I think I'll stay right here in hell.

MEURICE (*turning to leave*):   Kind of a bleak point of view there, isn't it Marty?

MARTY: Meurice . . .

MEURICE *pauses in the doorway.*

    . . . I don't want that asshole near my money. I don't even want him in the bar.

MEURICE: We get a lot of assholes in here, Marty.

MEURICE *and* DEBRA *can be heard leaving the bar.* MARTY *looks down at the telephone in front of him on the desk, then picks up the receiver and dials. He tilts back in his chair and stares back up at the ceiling.*

MARTY'S POV

The ceiling fan, turning slowly.

EXT   RAY'S BUNGALOW FROM INSIDE RAY'S CAR

In the foreground RAY *sits behind the wheel of his parked car, slumped back against the seat. He is staring at his one-story bungalow, in which a couple of lights are burning. Inside we can faintly hear his telephone ringing.*
    It rings for a long time.

RAY'S LIVING ROOM
CLOSE SHOT   THE RINGING TELEPHONE

ABBY's *hand enters frame, hesitates, then after another ring picks up.*

ABBY: Hello?

There is no answer. From the other end we hear only the rhythmic whir of a ceiling fan.

MARTY'S OFFICE

MARTY *listens. He says nothing, still tilted back in his chair, staring at the ceiling.*

RAY'S LIVING ROOM

ABBY *listens. She shifts the phone to her other ear, listening hard to the sound of the fan. There is another long pause.*

ABBY: . . . Marty?

The phone goes dead just as we hear the front door opening.
ABBY *looks up as she cradles the phone.*
    RAY *is standing in the doorway.*

RAY: Who was it?

ABBY: What?

RAY: On the phone. Was it for you?

Frances McDormand (Abby)

ABBY: I don't know, he didn't say anything.

RAY: Uh-huh. So how do you know it was a he?

ABBY (*smiling*):   You got a girl—am I screwing something up by being here?

> RAY *leans against the door and folds his arms, watching* ABBY.

RAY: No, am I?

> ABBY *looks at him, puzzled. After an uncomfortable pause:*

ABBY: . . . I can find a place tomorrow, then I'll be outta your hair.

RAY: If that's what you want to do, then you oughta do it. You, uh . . . you want the bed or the couch?

ABBY *shifts uneasily, looking at* RAY.

ABBY: Well . . . the couch would be all right . . .

RAY: You can sleep on the bed if you want.

ABBY: Well . . . I'm not gonna put you out of your bed . . .

RAY: You wouldn't be putting me out.

ABBY: . . . Well, I'd be okay in here—

RAY *walks toward the bedroom.*

RAY: Okay.

MARTY'S OFFICE   LATER

Still tilted back in his chair, MARTY *stares glumly at the ceiling. The bar itself is completely still except for the rhythmic whir of the fan.*

CLOSE SHOT   A CEILING FAN

Turning slowly. We tilt down from the fan to frame ABBY, *lying under a sheet on* RAY's *couch, staring up at the fan in the darkened living room. The room is still. We hear only the whir of the fan and the distant sound of crickets.* ABBY *turns her head, looking offscreen.*

HER POV

A ray of light slants up the hallway from the direction of the bedroom. The light is snapped off, leaving the hallway in darkness. We hear a faint cough and the creaking of bedsprings.

RAY'S BEDROOM

RAY lies in bed, staring at the ceiling.

RAY'S LIVING ROOM/HALLWAY
LONG SHOT   THE LIVING ROOM   FROM THE HALLWAY

ABBY sits up. She stands and walks across the moonlit room toward the hallway. We pull her back down the hall toward the bedroom. She pauses in the bedroom doorway and looks down toward the bed.

ABBY'S POV

RAY in bed, his eyes closed.

BACK TO ABBY

We pull her as she enters the room, then tilt down with her as she hesitantly sits on the edge of the bed.

ABBY'S POV

Close shot, RAY asleep.

BACK TO ABBY

Framed against a moonlit window from the shoulders up.
  There is a long pause.
  RAY's hand enters frame and pulls ABBY down out of frame onto the bed. We hold on the moonlit window.

DISSOLVE THROUGH TO:
SAME WINDOW   SAME ANGLE   PRE-DAWN

Through the window the slow dissolve gradually defines the front lawn and the street beyond in the flat pre-dawn light. ABBY rises into frame and quietly gets out of bed. The camera tracks behind her as she walks up the hallway into the living room.
  We follow her across the living room and move into a close

*shot on her hand as she reaches into her purse and withdraws
a small plastic compact.*

LOW-ANGLE CLOSE SHOT   ABBY

*She flips open the compact, then, hearing something, looks
up, squinting across the room.*

ABBY'S POV

*In the shadows at the far end of the room we can just see two
pointed ears and a glittering pair of eyes. The German
shepherd is panting softly.*

OVER ABBY'S SHOULDER

*As she peers into the shadows, her face reflected in the mirror
of the open compact.*

ABBY: Opal—

In the mirror something moves just behind her. ABBY *starts
to turn.*
      MARTY's *hand clamps over her mouth from behind. His
other hand circles her waist.* ABBY *struggles.*

MARTY (*quietly*):   Lover-boy oughta lock his door . . .

MARTY's *hand drops from her waist to her thighs and slides
under the robe.*

. . . Lotta nuts out there.

Still holding her from behind, MARTY *forces her down on her
knees.* ABBY's *cries are muffled by the hand clamped over her
mouth.* MARTY *shoots a glance down the dark hallway. There
is no movement.*
      ABBY's *hand is groping forward out of frame.*

CLOSE SHOT   ABBY'S PURSE

She upsets it. The contents spill out, among them a small pearl-handled revolver. Her hand gropes for the gun.

BACK TO ABBY AND MARTY

MARTY *yanks her to her feet, looking down the hallway.*

MARTY: Let's do it outside . . .

He is dragging her to the front door.

. . . in nature.

He pushes her through the screen door.

EXT   RAY'S BUNGALOW

The neighborhood is deserted and still. The streetlamps are still on. MARTY *and* ABBY *stumble down the front stoop onto the lawn.*
   His hand is still clamped over her mouth. She reaches up, grabs a finger, and bends it back.
   We hear the bone snap.
   MARTY *screams. His hand drops. His other hand cuffs her on the side of the head, spinning her around.*
   MARTY *is now clutching his broken finger with his good hand.* ABBY *kicks him in the groin.*
   He sinks to his knees, drops forward on one hand, and vomits.

FRONT STOOP

RAY *is coming out the door, hitching up his pants. In his right hand he holds* ABBY's *pearl-handled revolver.*

MARTY

Slowly gets to his feet, looking at RAY.

ABBY

She has backed away from MARTY *and now stands on the lawn, breathing heavily. She looks from* RAY *to* MARTY.

BACK TO MARTY

Backing toward his car, a Cadillac parked at curbside, still looking at RAY. *He turns to get into the car.*

The German shepherd lopes across the lawn and takes a clean leap into the car through the open window on the passenger side.

MARTY *turns the ignition. The engine coughs and dies. He tries again; it starts.*

The car roars up the street.

RAY

Watching the car. He looks at ABBY.

ABBY

Still panting. Up the street we can hear MARTY's *car braking and grinding gears.*

RAY *enters to embrace* ABBY. *We hear* MARTY's *car alternately racing and stopping, shifting in and out of gear. His engine rumble starts to grow louder again.*

RAY: Like to have seen his face when he found the dead end.

In the background we see MARTY's *car roar by in the opposite direction.*

MOUNT BONNEL.   EVENING
LATERAL TRACK

Moving past a row of cars parked on an overlook near the top of the mountain. Below we can see the lights of the city of Austin. The lot is littered with beer cans. We hear the sound of rock music coming from various car radios. Several teenagers lean against cars drinking beer; inside the cars we can see the vague forms of others.

TEENAGER: Hey mister, how'd you break your pussy-finger?

His friends laugh.

TRACK PULLING MARTY

Ignoring the laughter as he walks past the cars, apparently looking for someone. His right index finger is taped up in an aluminum splint.

MARTY'S POV

At the end of a row of cars we see a green Volkswagen bug. Leaning against the hood is VISSER, *still dressed in his rumpled yellow suit. He is smoking a cigarette, talking to a sixteen-year-old girl in shorts and a tube top. When he notices* MARTY:

VISSER *(to the girl)*:   Sorry sweetheart, my date is here . . .

The girl drifts off. MARTY *enters frame and* VISSER *turns to him.*

. . . She saw me rolling a cigarette and thought it was marijuana *(he laughs)*. I guess she thought I was a swinger.

VISSER *opens the back door of the car.* MARTY *ignores the invitation, walks around to the front door on the passenger side and gets in.*

INT VISSER'S CAR

As VISSER *gets into the driver's seat. A small topless doll is suspended from the rearview mirror.* VISSER *gives it a tap. As it swings back and forth two small lights, one behind each breast, blink on and off.*

VISSER: Idnat wild?

Both men sit watching the doll intently.
    Finally MARTY *reaches up and stops its swinging with the rounded end of his splint.* VISSER *eyes the splint.*

VISSER (*genially*):   Stick your finger up the wrong person's ass?

MARTY *is silent, but* VISSER *is in a good mood.*

VISSER: You know a friend of mine broke his hand a while back. Put in a cast. Very next day he takes a fall, protects his bad hand, falls on his good one, breaks that too. So now he's got two busted flippers and I say to him "Creighton, I hope your wife loves you. 'Cause for the next five weeks you cannot wipe your own goddamn ass . . ."

Overcome by laughter. Finally:

. . . That's the test, ain't it? Test of true love—

MARTY: Got a job for you.

VISSER (*settling down*):   . . . Well, if the pay's right and it's legal I'll do it.

MARTY: It's not strictly legal.

VISSER shrugs, lights up another cigarette with his fraternally inscribed lighter and drops the lighter onto the dashboard.

VISSER: If the pay's right I'll do it.

MARTY: It's, uh . . . it's in reference to that gentleman and my wife. The more I think about it the more irritated I get.

VISSER: Yeah? Well how irritated are you?

MARTY doesn't answer. Finally VISSER laughs.

. . . Gee, I'm sorry to hear that. Can you tell me what you want me to do or is it a secret?

MARTY: Listen, I'm not—this isn't a joke here.

VISSER eyes him, still smiling. Finally he shrugs.

VISSER: You want me to kill 'em.

MARTY: I didn't say that (*a pause*). . . . Well?

VISSER: Well what?

MARTY: What do you think?

VISSER: You're an idiot.

MARTY's shoulders slump. He seems less tense, almost relieved.

MARTY: So, uh . . . this wouldn't interest you.

VISSER: I didn't say that. All I said was you're an idiot. Hell, you been thinking about it so much it's driving you simple.

They are staring at each other.

MARTY: Ten thousand dollars I'll give you.

VISSER laughs again.

VISSER: I'm supposed to do a murder—two murders— and just trust you not to go simple on me and do something stupid. I mean real stupid. Now why should I trust you?

MARTY: For the money.

VISSER (*sobering*): The money. Yeah. That's a right smart of money . . .

He turns and gazes out the window.

. . . In Russia they make only fifty cent a day.

*He falls silent again, still staring out the window.
In the closeness of the car MARTY is starting to sweat.*

MARTY (*hoarsely*): . . . There's a big—

VISSER (*abruptly*): I want you to go fishing.

MARTY: . . . What?

VISSER: Go down to Corpus for a few days. Get yourself noticed. I'll give you a call when it's done . . . You just find a way to cover that money.

MARTY *is slumped in his seat, not responding to the fact that* VISSER *has just ended the conversation.*

Finally he rouses himself and gets out of the car, leaving VISSER *staring at the door he has left open behind him.*

After a moment we hear MARTY*'s footsteps approaching again, and he leans back into the open door with an afterthought.*

MARTY: I'll take care of the money, you just make sure those bodies aren't found . . . There's a . . .

These words are difficult to say.

. . . If you want, there's a big incinerator behind my place . . .

The two men look at each other. MARTY *leaves. After a moment,* VISSER *leans over to grab the handle of the still open door.*

VISSER (*under his breath*):   Sweet Jesus, you are disgusting.

The door slams.

INT EMPTY APARTMENT NIGHT

The apartment is dark. We are looking across a shadowy floor towards a large window, through which cold blue street light shines. Through the window we can see the facade of the building across the street; we are three or four floors up.

We can hear the animated, accented voice of an Hispanic woman approaching the apartment from the hallway behind us.

LANDLADY (*os*):   —big windows, paneleen and everytheen. So you want, like your own place? Like a Town House?

*A crack of light shoots across the floor as we hear the
apartment door open behind us. A figure enters frame. As it
crosses into the shaft of light we see that it is ABBY. She
moves across the dark apartment, in silhouette against the
window.*

LANDLADY (*os*): No one will bother you here, sweetie—

*An overhead light is switched on and the room is bathed in
light. Several feet from ABBY, an old man in a dirty
undershirt is asleep on a cot. ABBY starts.*
   The old man grumbles, slowly sits up, squints.
   *With the light, the window behind ABBY has become a
mirror of the entire room, in which we now see the matronly
LANDLADY standing by the wall switch.*
   *The LANDLADY roars at the old man in Spanish. The man
glowers at her. The LANDLADY looks back at ABBY.*

LANDLADY (*cheerful again*): I show you around.

*We follow ABBY as she accompanies the landlady back into the
short hallway–entrance foyer. ABBY glances back at the old
man.*

ABBY: Are you sure this is . . . Are you sure this
apartment is vacant? . . . Mrs. Esteves?

The LANDLADY laughs cheerfully.

LANDLADY: Oh yes . . .

She gestures to a kitchen alcove on the left.

. . . That's the kitchen . . .

*She turns and throws a few more barbs in Spanish back
toward the old man, then opens a door on the right side of the
foyer and enters the bathroom.*

. . . This is the bathroom . . .

She flushes the toilet.

. . . The toilet works and everytheen . . .

She bustles out of the bathroom and takes the two short steps back into the main room. She gestures expansively.

. . . And here we are back in the liveen room.

She gives one vigorous stomp.

. . . Good floors. Gas heat.

She points.

. . . That's Mr. Garcia.

The old man is now sitting on the edge of the bed, smoking a cigarette, looking for a place to put the ash. The LANDLADY *snaps at him again in Spanish, and is again cheerful as she turns back to address* ABBY.

. . . I was just esplaineen to him that he moved out of here yesterday . . .

She walks toward the apartment door.

. . . You look around. Don't mind Mr. Garcia; he use do be my brother-in-law.

She walks out and shuts the door.
The room is quiet.

CLOSE SHOT   ABBY

Staring at the door. She looks at MR. GARCIA, *looks nervously around the apartment. She looks back at* MR. GARCIA.

CLOSE SHOT   MR. GARCIA

Staring vacantly at ABBY. *He blows a stream of smoke across the room. The ash falls off his cigarette.*

STRIP BAR   NIGHT
EXHORTER'S CUBICLE

Hunched over the public address microphone in his small cubicle of exhortation, is the middle-aged strip-bar barker. Years of service in the bar have left his exhortations depressingly bereft of conviction.

EXHORTER: How 'bout it, gentlemen, let's show our appreciation for Lorraine up there, a registered nurse from Bolton, Texas, how 'bout it gentlemen, yeah . . .

THE BAR PROPER

MEURICE *is one of a line of men sitting at the bar, all looking intently at the same point off left. All of the men except* MEURICE *are conservatively dressed and apparently well-to-do. An audio loop is blaring a bump-and-grind version of "Yellow Rose of Texas," punctuated by the crash of cymbals and the thumping of toms.*
    ABBY *enters and sits into an empty chair next to* MEURICE.

ABBY: Looks like the state legislature is out of session.

MEURICE *continues to stare intently off.*

MEURICE: I thought this was where they met.

All of the heads at the bar start to swivel, including MEURICE'*s. A couple of patrons hurriedly snatch their drinks off the bar.*
    In the extreme foreground a stripper dances on top of the bar into frame. We crop her just above her white high-heeled cowboy boots and her bare calves.

Frances McDormand, seated at far left, and Samm-Art Williams
(Meurice), second from left

The conversation continues with ABBY *looking at*
MEURICE, *but* MEURICE *and everyone else at the bar looking
up at a point somewhere above the stripper's bare calves.*

ABBY: Listen Meurice, you're gonna help me with a
problem.

MEURICE: I am?

*The stripper drops a white leatherette vest onto the bar in the
foreground. The audience cheers.*

ABBY: You're gonna keep an eye on Marty and Ray,
make sure nothing happens.

MEURICE: It won't?

*Two sheriff-star pasties drop onto the bar. The audience
cheers.*

. . . Ever occur to you, Abby, that maybe I'm the wrong person to ask?

THE EXHORTER

Into his microphone.

EXHORTER: Let's not sit on our wallets, gentlemen. Lorraine is up there dancing her heart out, and if you let that cash money set on your hip, you might just as well be broke . . .

ABBY AND MEURICE

She is rising to leave; he is still staring off.

ABBY: Thanks, Meurice.

MEURICE: Any time. But you don't have to worry about a thing for a while. Marty went down to Corpus yesterday.

An old-west gunbelt hits the bar. The audience roars.

THE EXHORTER

Into his microphone.

EXHORTER: And remember, gentlemen, we're always here, two to two, A.M. to P.M., three hundred and sixty-four days and Christmas, God willing and the creek don't rise . . .

RAY'S BEDROOM

The room is dark. We are looking across the room toward a moonlit window. Beyond, across the lawn, the lamplit street is empty.
  Suddenly ABBY *sits bolt upright into frame from the bed below.*

ABBY: He's in the house.

Offscreen we hear RAY *stirring in bed.*

RAY: What's the matter?

ABBY *twists around to look down at him.*

ABBY: I could've sworn I heard something.

RAY: Door's locked. Nothing there.

He pulls her down out of frame and we hold on the window and the empty lamplit street. Then ABBY *rises back into frame, in silhouette against the window, looking down at* RAY.

ABBY: I knew it. 'Cause we wouldn't have heard anything if it was him. He's real careful. Fact is, he's anal.

RAY: . . . Huh?

ABBY: Yeah, he told me once himself. He said to me . . .

She taps herself on the forehead.

. . . "In here, Abby. In here . . . I'm anal."

HIGH ANGLE   RAY
Looking up at Abby.

RAY (*yawning*):   . . . Well I'll be damned.

ABBY: I couldn't believe it either . . .

SIDE ANGLE   ABBY

Framed against the window, looking down at RAY.

ABBY: . . . Me on the other hand, I got lots of
personality . . .

*She drops down onto the bed out of frame. The camera holds
on the window through which we see the empty lamplit
street.*

ABBY: Marty always said I had too much. 'Course he
was never big on personality . . .

*She rises back up into frame, in silhouette against the
window.*

. . . He sent me to a psychiatrist to see if he could calm
me down some.

RAY: Yeah? What happened?

ABBY: Psychiatrist said I was the healthiest person he'd
ever met, so Marty fired him.

RAY *(sleepily)*:   . . . I don't know if you can fire a
psychiatrist, exactly.

ABBY: Well, I didn't see him anymore, I'll tell you that
much.

HIGH ANGLE   RAY

His eyes half-closed.

RAY: Uh-huh.

ABBY: I said, Marty, how come *you're* anal and *I* gotta go to the psychiatrist?

RAY: What'd he say?

SIDE ANGLE   ABBY

Framed against the window.

ABBY: Nothing. He's like you, he doesn't say much.

RAY (*murmuring*):   Thanks.

ABBY: Except when he doesn't say things they're usually nasty.

RAY: . . . Mm-hmm.

ABBY: When you don't they're usually nice.

RAY: . . . You ever get tired?

ABBY: Huh? Oh, yeah, I guess. Mm-hmm.

RAY's *hand rises into frame and coaxes* ABBY *back down onto the bed, revealing, through the window, a green Volkswagen now parked at curbside on the lamplit street.*
    We hear the rustle of sheets.
    As we hold on the window, we begin to hear the faint, distant sound of metal scraping against metal.

HALLWAY/LIVING ROOM

We track down the dark hallway into the living room. As the camera advances the sound of the scraping becomes louder.
    We are moving across the living room up to the front door of the bungalow. The scraping is louder still as we finally frame on a close shot of the doorknob, which is jiggling ever so slightly.

We hear a click as the lock finally releases.
The door swings slowly open, revealing a man's hand on the outside doorknob. We follow the hand as the man advances slowly and quietly across the living room.
ABBY's purse comes into frame, sitting on a bureau; next to it is a large tote bag. The hand rummages through the tote bag briefly, then the purse. The man withdraws ABBY's pearl-handled revolver. He breaks it open.

LOW-ANGLE CLOSE SHOT　THE MAN'S FACE

It is VISSER. As we hear a click offscreen, his face glows a dim orange.

BACK TO HIS HANDS

His right holds the revolver, cylinder open, inside the purse. His left holds his cigarette lighter as he inspects the chamber. Three of the holes glint silver, the other three are black— empty.
We hear the faint creaking of bedsprings.

WIDE SHOT　LIVING ROOM

VISSER cocks his head, listening, and looks down the. hallway. He takes a couple of quiet steps across the living room and, as the camera tracks up to him, opens the back door of the bungalow.
We follow him outside onto the lawn.

EXT　RAY'S BUNGALOW

We track behind him as he rounds the corner of the house and approaches the open window to RAY's bedroom. He slows, moves more cautiously, then sinks to his knees under the window. As he reaches into his breast pocket the camera continues tracking up to and over him, finally framing his POV through the window.
On the bed inside we can dimly see ABBY and RAY, asleep.
We have been hearing a faint rumble, becoming louder and

louder as if approaching from a distance. Just as the rumble becomes deafening a sudden bright flash of light illuminates the room, seeming to polarize the image of ABBY *and* RAY *in bed, and we:*

CUT TO:
EXT   PHONE BOOTH   DAY

A huge truck roars by on the street behind VISSER, *and with it the deafening rumble recedes. It is a painfully bright day.* VISSER *stands sweating in the phone booth with the receiver pressed to his ear. We hear the phone ringing at the other end.*
  Finally, it is picked up.

VOICE: Hello.

VISSER: Marty?

MARTY: Yeah. Is it . . .

VISSER: Ya catch any fish?

M. Emmet Walsh (Visser)

MARTY: . . . What?

VISSER: Ya catch any fish?

MARTY: Yeah . . .

VISSER: . . . What kind of fish?

MARTY: Listen, what is it? Is it done?

VISSER forces a chuckle.

VISSER: . . . Yessir, you owe me some money.

MARTY'S OFFICE   NIGHT
CLOSE SHOT   TWO STRINGS OF FISH

Being plopped down onto MARTY's desk.

WIDER   THE OFFICE

VISSER sits facing the desk. He lights himself a cigarette and sets the lighter down on the desk in front of him. MARTY settles, fidgeting, into the chair behind it.
The bar is quiet, shut down. We hear only the whir of a fan somewhere offscreen. MARTY and VISSER are lit by a lamp on the desk between them. Light streams into the room from a bathroom in the background. VISSER is looking at the dead fish.

VISSER (*dully*):   They look good.

MARTY half-rises from his seat and picks up one of the strings.

MARTY: Want a couple?

He drops them on VISSER's side of the desk. VISSER's head draws back: he was only being polite.

VISSER: Just the ten thousand'll be fine.

MARTY: Got something to show me first?

VISSER hands a 9 × 12 envelope across the desk. MARTY stares at it for a moment, then quickly bends back the flap and takes out an 8 × 10 photograph.

THE PHOTOGRAPH

It is a black-and-white shot of ABBY and RAY in RAY's bed. The sheet that partially covers them is pocked with three dark bullet holes and is stained with blood.

MARTY

Staring dully down at the picture.

MARTY: Dead, huh?

VISSER: So it would seem.

CLOSE SHOT   THE TOP OF THE DESK

VISSER is pushing the fish away from his side of the desk with the eraser end of a pencil.

MARTY: What did you . . .

BACK TO MARTY

Still looking at the picture. He traces the outline of ABBY's body with his finger.

MARTY: . . . What did you do with the bodies?

VISSER: It's taken care of. The less you know about it the better.

MARTY: Jesus, I don't believe it . . .

MARTY *slips the picture back into its 9 × 12 envelope. His face is pale.*

MARTY: . . . I think I'm gonna be sick.

He rises and heads for the bathroom, still clutching the envelope.

CLOSE SHOT   VISSER

As his eyes follow MARTY's *exit. The bathroom door doesn't close all the way: a narrow shaft of light slices the office from the bare bulb in the bathroom.*

VISSER: I'll want that picture back . . .

He turns to look across the desk.

VISSER'S POV

The standing safe behind the desk.

BACK TO VISSER

Still looking at the safe. Beads of sweat have popped out on his forehead. He fans himself with his cowboy hat.

VISSER: . . . and you did say somethin' about some money.

We hear a toilet flush offscreen.

LONG SHOT   MARTY

As he reenters the office.

MARTY: Your money, yeah.

VISSER *stares dully down at the desktop.*

VISSER: Something I got to ask you, Marty. I been very very careful. Have you been very very careful?

MARTY: Of course.

VISSER: Nobody knows you hired me?

HIGH ANGLE   CORNER OF THE OFFICE

MARTY is hunched over the open safe, still holding the envelope. Blocking VISSER's view of the safe with his body, he slides the picture of ABBY's and RAY's corpses from under the envelope into the safe, then withdraws two packets of money.

MARTY: Don't be absurd, I wasn't about to tell anyone . . .

He shuts the safe and spins the dial.

. . . This is an illicit romance—we've got to trust each other to be discreet . . .

He walks across the room and throws the money and the envelope down on the desk.

. . . For richer, for poorer.

VISSER looks from the money down at his hands. They are sweating.

VISSER: Don't say that. Your marriages don't work out so hot . . .

He wipes his hands on his pants.

. . . How did you cover the money?

MARTY sits and props his booted feet up on the desk.

MARTY: It's taken care of. The less you know about it the better.

He smiles.

. . . I just made a call about that. It'll look fine.

VISSER (*shaking his head*):   I must've gone money simple. This kind of murder . . .

He nods toward the envelope on the desk.

. . . it's too damn risky.

MARTY: Then you shouldn't have done it. Can't have it both ways.

He pushes the money across the desk with his boot.

. . . Count it if you want.

VISSER (*reaching into his coat*):   Nah, I trust ya.

His hand comes out with a gun pointing at MARTY and—BAM—he fires, an orange lick of flame spurting from the gun.
   Both men sit frozen. VISSER's hand is the only thing that moved.

CLOSE SHOT   MARTY

Staring at VISSER.
   After the gun blast we hear only the whir of the fan.

CLOSE SHOT   VISSER

Staring at MARTY.

MED SHOT   MARTY   OVER VISSER'S SHOULDER

His eyes are now shut. Otherwise he hasn't moved. A blood stain is growing on the front of his shirt.

WIDE SHOT   THE OFFICE

The two face each other across the desk. VISSER's gun is still trained on MARTY.

After a moment VISSER starts fanning himself again with his cowboy hat. The only movement in the frame is the slow back-and-forth of the yellow hat, rhythmically in and out of shadow as it catches and loses the light from the desk lamp. There is a long pause.

Finally one of MARTY's feet slips from the desk and hits the floor with a THUD.

VISSER lays the gun on the desk.

CLOSE SHOT   VISSER

As he reaches into his breast pocket and withdraws a handkerchief. He wipes his forehead, then picks up the gun and wipes it off. He leans down with the gun.

CLOSE SHOT   THE GUN

As VISSER places it deliberately on the floor near the desk. It is ABBY's pearl-handled revolver.

THE DESKTOP   FROM DESK LEVEL

As VISSER straightens up in the foreground. From our head-on angle shooting across the desk we can see the bright metallic glint of VISSER's cigarette lighter underneath the dead fish.

VISSER's hands move over the near part of the desk, picking up the money and the 9 × 12 picture envelope.

EXTREME HIGH SHOT   THE OFFICE

As VISSER turns from the desk and walks across the room out of frame. We hear the back door opening.

VISSER: Who looks stupid now.

The door slams shut.
The only sound is the whir of the fan. A pause. The camera tracks slowly forward, tilting down to keep MARTY *and the desktop centered in frame. As the camera moves the noise of the fan grows louder. When* MARTY's *body and the desk are directly beneath us, the blades of the ceiling fan cut across the immediate foreground and effect a:*

WIPE TO:
MARTY'S BAR LATER

It is completely still. We are looking from the bar, across the dark empty floor, toward the pebbled windows at the front of the building that catch a hard blue light from the streetlamps outside. The jukebox in the middle distance glows in the darkness.

A pair of headlights catches the pebbled glass and grows brighter as we hear a car pull up to the bar and stop. We hear a car door open and shut, then the sound of feet on gravel. A huge shadow appears on the pebbled glass as the figure crosses in front of the headlights. The man tries the door, finds it locked, and walks back in front of the headlights to cup his hands at a window. He walks back to the door, and a moment later it swings open—framing him in the doorway in silhouette.

We follow him as he moves across the floor, behind the bar and up to the cash register. He switches on a small fluorescent light clamped to the top of the cash register. It is RAY.

He punches a key and the register rings open. He lifts up the empty cash drawer and takes some papers from underneath it.

RAY'S POV

As he flips through the papers: bills, receipts, no money.

BACK TO RAY

As he finishes flipping through the papers.

RAY (*muttering*):   Damn . . .

He slips them back under the cash drawer and slams the register shut. Turning from the register he glances around the bar, then pauses, noticing something.

RAY'S POV

Light is spilling out from under the door to MARTY's *office.*

BACK TO RAY

As he starts across the floor to MARTY's *office.*

RAY: Marty . . .

He reaches the door and knocks sharply. No answer. He turns the knob.

. . . Marty.

The door is locked. We hear the muffled whir of the ceiling fan inside.
    A pause. RAY *withdraws a ring of keys from his pocket and uses one on the door. The door swings open.*
    Over his shoulder we see MARTY, *still at his desk, his back to us. One foot is still propped on the desk.*

RAY: What's the matter, you deaf?

No answer.
    RAY *starts toward* MARTY.
    He stumbles slightly and we hear the sharp blast of a gun and the sound of something metallic skating across the floor.
    RAY, *startled, steadies himself against the desk, then studies* MARTY.

RAY'S POV

There is a dark pool of blood under MARTY's *chair.*

BACK TO RAY

He looks back up at MARTY, *then walks behind his chair and throws a wall switch. The room is bathed in light. His eyes still on* MARTY, RAY *crosses behind the desk.*

RAY'S POV   TRACKING SHOT

The camera moves in a slow arc around the back of MARTY'S *motionless head.*

BACK TO RAY

Still moving. He looks away from MARTY, *scans the floor. He gets down on his hands and knees and peers under the safe.*

RAY'S POV

There is a glinting silver circle in the darkness under the safe. It is the business end of the revolver that RAY *half-stumbled over, half-kicked.*

BACK TO RAY

Still on his hands and knees. He reaches in and we hear a rattle as he gropes under the safe. He withdraws the gun, looks at it.

THE GUN

It is ABBY'S *revolver.*

BACK TO RAY

For a long moment he doesn't move. Then, slowly, he starts to get up.

WIDER

The desk, MARTY *behind it,* RAY *straightening behind him.* RAY *looks from the gun to* MARTY, *slowly sets the gun down on the desk. A pause. He begins to hoist* MARTY *from the chair.*

There is noise from the bar, as of someone entering.
RAY *reacts.*

THE DOOR

Separating the bar and back office. RAY *hurries to it.*

MEURICE (*os*):   Marty?

Footsteps approach the door.

EXTREME CLOSE SHOT   RAY'S HAND ON THE DOOR BOLT

He turns it gently. The bolt clicks shut.

BACK TO RAY

MEURICE's *footsteps draw nearer.*

MEURICE (*os*):   Marty, ya home?

There is a rap at the door; RAY *stands frozen. The doorknob rattles.* RAY *reaches out compulsively to grab it, but stops himself before actually touching it.*
   Now MEURICE's *footsteps can be heard going casually back into the bar. We hold on* RAY's *rigidly set face.*

MEURICE (*os*):   What day is it today, Angie?

WOMAN (*os*):   Tuesday.

MEURICE (*os*):   Tuesday night is ladies' night.

WOMAN (*os*):   What?

MEURICE (*os*):   Tuesday night is ladies' night. All your drinks are free.

We hear a record drop on the jukebox and a Motown song
blares.

RAY crosses to MARTY's chair and takes off his nylon
windbreaker. He stoops down and tries to mop up the pool of
blood with his windbreaker. This isn't going to work.

He rises and walks over to the bathroom, the windbreaker
dripping blood.

MARTY'S OFFICE BATHROOM
CLOSE SHOT FAUCET

The song continues faintly in the background. The faucet is
turned on and RAY's hand enters frame, holding a dirty white
towel under the stream of water.

BLOOD-SPATTERED FLOOR

The song continues in the background. RAY's hand enters
frame holding the balled-up towel. His windbreaker is
wrapped inside. The camera follows as he pushes it across the
trail of dripped blood to the pool of blood under MARTY's
chair.

CLOSE SHOT MARTY

He still has not moved. RAY rises into frame and takes him
under the armpits. He notices something on the desk in front
of him.

CLOSE SHOT THE GUN ON THE DESK

RAY's hand enters frame and picks it up.

CLOSE SHOT MARTY'S COAT POCKET

RAY's hand enters frame and slips the gun into MARTY's
pocket. MARTY is hoisted up.

EXT BACK OF THE BAR/PARKING LOT

RAY appears in the doorway. The music from the bar, though
fainter, can still be heard.

There are three or four wooden steps going down from the
back door to the small gravel parking lot in back. RAY backs
down the stairs; MARTY's feet THUMP-THUMP-THUMP
down the stairs after him.
   The rear door of RAY's car is open. RAY heaves in MARTY's
torso. MARTY's legs rest on the ground outside the car. RAY
takes an ankle in each hand and pushes.

CLOSE SHOT   RAY

As he shuts the back door. He looks up across the parking lot.

RAY'S POV

The incinerator belching fire and smoke. We hear its distant
roar over the bar song. We hear the car door slam.

**HIGH-ANGLE TRACKING SHOT   TOWARD
INCINERATOR**

We are looking down on RAY's car as the camera tracks
behind it towards the incinerator. At the cut the roar of the
incinerator is suddenly louder. It grows louder still as we
approach it.
   RAY's car draws even with the incinerator without slowing
or stopping. The wadded-up towel is chucked out of his
window into the fire. We hold on the fire as RAY's car rolls on
out of frame.

INT   RAY'S CAR

As he drives down a deserted country highway. We hear the
rhythmic sound of the wheels clomping over asphalt. The
radio is broadcasting a fundamentalist's sermon, periodically
interrupted by static. RAY is sweating.

EVANGELIST: —so there were three signs, the second of
which is Famine, this famine which I have already
pointed out is devastatin' Africa and the Indian

subcontinent. And the third of these signs is earthquakes. Now I don't know why he threw that in but if you talk to a geologist, and I've talked to many, he'll tell you that earthquake activity—

RAY *twists around and looks in the back seat.*

RAY'S POV

MARTY *is lying inert.*

—has increased almost eighty percent in the past two years, and what's more, in two years' time we'll be experiencin' what's known as the Jupiter Effect—

BACK TO RAY

He looks back at the road. A car roars by.

—wherein all the planets of the known universe will be aligned up causin' an incredible buildup of destructive gravitational force. Now in Matthew Chapter Six, Verse Eighteen the Lord out and tells us that these are the signs by which we shall know that He is at our door. There are many good people disagree with me, but it's my belief that this Antichrist is alive today and livin' somewhere in Europe, in that ten-nation alliance I spoke of, bein' groomed for his task—

RAY *switches off the radio.*
We hear the sound of faint, labored breathing.

EXTREME CLOSE SHOT   RAY

His jaw tightens. He whips his head toward the back seat.
His head snaps forward again and he slams on the brakes.
The car screeches to a halt.

EXT   HIGHWAY
LONG SHOT   THE CAR

As RAY's door flies open. He is bolting from the car. The camera, at waist level, tracks toward him as he races out into the field that abuts the highway.

Fifty yards in he finally stops, panting, framed from a low angle. His breath vaporizes in the crisp night air. We hear only his breath and the chirring of crickets. He is looking back toward the road.

RAY'S POV   LONG SHOT   THE CAR

Standing abandoned on the shoulder of the deserted highway. Its headlights cast a lonely beam up the road. No movement.

BACK TO RAY

His panting slows. He is in a cold sweat. After a long moment, he starts walking slowly, reluctantly, back toward the car.

RAY'S POV   TRACKING

Toward the car. Still no sign of movement.

BACK TO RAY

He slows as he draws up to the back of the car. He looks in the back window.

RAY'S POV   BACK SEAT OF THE CAR

It is empty.
The door on the highway side is ajar.

BACK TO RAY

No reaction.
He walks around the back of the car onto the highway. He looks up the road.

RAY'S POV

MARTY *is crawling up the road on his hands and knees,*
leaving a trail of blood. The headlights of RAY's *car give him a*
fantastically long shadow.

BACK TO RAY

Still no reaction. He gets into the driver's seat and stares
through the windshield as he gropes for the ignition key.

RAY'S POV

MARTY, *crawling.*

BACK TO RAY

He throws the car into drive, looks at his target, thinks—
decides. He pulls the key out of the ignition and goes around
to the trunk of the car. He opens it and pulls out a shovel.

MARTY   LOW ANGLE

From in front. The headlights glare behind him. His breath
vaporizes. In the background RAY *is walking toward him,*
dragging the shovel, which scrapes along the asphalt. As RAY
moves into the foreground and turns to face MARTY *only his*
lower legs and the shovel are in frame.
   The shovel rises out of frame.

CLOSE SHOT   RAY

Both hands hold the shovel tensed over his shoulder. He
stares down at MARTY. *A long pause. We hear a distant*
rumble.

CLOSE SHOT   RAY'S FEET

Inches away from MARTY. MARTY's *hand slides forward and*
wraps around one of RAY's *ankles.*

BACK TO RAY

He shudders. He adjusts his grip on the shovel.
The rumble grows louder.

RAY'S FEET

He jerks his foot away, breaking MARTY'*s grasp.*

BACK TO RAY

Looks up from MARTY. *The rumble grows louder.*

RAY'S POV

Headlight beams, although not yet the headlights themselves,
are visible a long way down the road.

BACK TO RAY

Staring down the road. Finally he lowers the shovel, walks
back to the car and throws it viciously into the trunk, walks
back up into the foreground and stoops down.

CLOSE SHOT   MARTY

As RAY *grabs him under the armpits and starts dragging him*
back to the car. Just before RAY *heaves him into the back seat,*
MARTY *coughs weakly. A fine spray of blood comes out with*
the cough.
The engine rumble is quite loud now.

MED SHOT   RAY   FROM ACROSS THE ROOF OF THE CAR

As he slams the back door shut. He presses himself against
the side of his car. Headlights glare over him; the truck roars
by just behind him.

EXT   OPEN FIELD
FULL SHOT   RAY'S CAR

Sudden quiet at the cut. We are looking at RAY'*s car in*
profile, parked in the middle of a deserted field. From

offscreen we hear the sound of a shovel biting into earth.
We track laterally down the car, along the beam of its
headlights, to finally frame RAY *as he climbs out of the*
shallow grave he has just finished digging.
He plants the shovel and walks back to the car.

VERY WIDE SHOT

The grave in the middle background; the car's headlights
beyond it.
RAY *is dragging* MARTY *toward the grave. He dumps him*
in.

HIGH SHOT   THE GRAVE

As MARTY *thumps to the bottom, face up.*

CLOSE SHOT   RAY

As he bends over to pick up the shovel, dripping sweat. We
hear the shovel biting into earth.

HIGH SHOT   THE GRAVE

RAY, *in the foreground, pitches the first shovelful of earth*
onto MARTY. MARTY *moves slightly.*

LOW SHOT   RAY

As he pauses, looking down into the grave. He stoops down
and resumes shoveling, bobbing in and out of frame as he
hurls dirt into the grave.

BACK TO HIGH SHOT

As RAY *shovels,* MARTY *is moving under the loose dirt. A*
faint, inarticulate noise comes from the grave.
Almost imperceptibly, MARTY's *right arm starts to rise.*

LOW SHOT   FROM INSIDE THE GRAVE

RAY *stands on the lip of the grave, hunched over his shovel,*
crisply illuminated by the headlights. In the shadowy

foreground MARTY's *arm rises, extended toward* RAY. *He is clutching* ABBY's *gun in his splint-fingered hand.*

CLOSE SHOT   RAY

As he straightens up and stands motionless, expressionless, watching MARTY, *making no attempt to get out of the way.*

HIGH SHOT   MARTY

The gun extended into the foreground. His index finger splinted, he slides his middle finger over the trigger of the gun.

LOW SHOT   RAY

Watching.

HIGH SHOT   MARTY

The gun trembling in the foreground. His knuckle whitens over the trigger.
   The trigger releases and we hear the dull click of an empty chamber.

LOW SHOT   RAY

Staring blankly down at MARTY.

SIDE SHOT

Of MARTY's *gun hand as* RAY *slowly sinks down on the lip of the grave, bracing himself with the shovel. His hand reaches for* MARTY's. MARTY *squeezes off two more empty chambers.* RAY's *hand slowly closes over the barrel of the gun.*
   As he pulls, the gun slides from MARTY's *fingers.*

CLOSE SHOT   THE BLADE OF THE SHOVEL

Biting into the earth.

MED SHOT   RAY

Furiously shoveling dirt into the grave.

HIGH SHOT   THE GRAVE

MARTY barely visible under the dirt.

MED SHOT   RAY

Shoveling, panting.

HIGH SHOT   THE GRAVE

Half full.

MED SHOT   RAY

Working furiously. His breath comes in short gasps.

HIGH SHOT   THE GRAVE

It is filled. RAY is packing down the earth, slamming the shovel furiously against the bare patch of earth.

CLOSE SHOT   THE BLADE OF THE SHOVEL

Being slammed down against the earth. Again and again.

EXT   OPEN FIELD   SUNRISE

The staccato beat of the shovel slamming against earth drops out at the cut. There is perfect quiet. The sun is just peeping over the horizon. In the foreground RAY is sitting in the open door of his car, smoking a cigarette. His gaze is fixed on a spot offscreen.

HIS POV

A house. Quite near by.
   The house and its perfect green rectangle of lawn are set incongruously in the middle of the open field.

BACK TO RAY

Staring, without emotion.

He takes one last, fierce drag on the cigarette, then flicks it away. He takes the shovel, walks over to the grave and stares at it for several seconds, shovel clasped firmly in both hands.

He walks back to the car.

HIGH SHOT

House, car and grave. RAY *throws the shovel into the car, gets in, and turns the ignition.*

The engine coughs weakly and dies.

He tries again. Same result.

One more time. The engine coughs, sputters, and fires to life. The car runs over the grave and rattles on across the rutted field towards the highway in the distance.

INT   RAY'S CAR   DAWN

As RAY *drives down the straight empty highway in the flat early-morning light.*

CLOSE SHOT   RAY

Pale and unblinking.

RAY'S POV   THE HIGHWAY

In the distance we see a beat-up white station wagon approaching. Its headlights wink on, then off again.

BACK TO RAY

He squints at the approaching car.

RAY'S POV

The car is closer. Its headlights wink again.

BACK TO RAY

His jaw tightens. He stares intently at the car. Then, abruptly, he looks down at his dashboard.

CLOSE SHOT   HEADLIGHT KNOB ON THE DASHBOARD

His headlights are on. RAY's *hand enters frame and pushes in the knob.*

SIDE ANGLE   RAY

Watching the approaching station wagon. As it passes we catch a glimpse of its occupant. He grins and cocks a you-got-it finger at RAY *before roaring on out of frame.*

EXT   DESERTED GAS STATION
HIGH ANGLE

The station hasn't opened yet. RAY's *car, empty, stands alone in the lot. Flat prairie stretches to the horizon. No movement in the frame.*

   At the cut we hear the faint sound of a phone ringing through a receiver. After four or five rings the phone is picked up and we begin a slow crane down.

ABBY (*through phone; sleepily*):   Hello?

RAY (*present; very hoarsely*):   Abby . . . you all right?

ABBY: Ray? . . . What time is it?

RAY: I don't know. It's early . . . I love you.

   A beat.

ABBY: . . . You all right?

RAY: I don't know. I better get off now.

   The continuing crane down reveals RAY *in a phone booth in the foreground.*

ABBY: Okay, see ya . . . Thanks, Ray.

RAY: Abby—

The phone disconnects.

INT ABBY'S APARTMENT
CLOSE SHOT ABBY

*Her sleeping head on a pillow. Offscreen we hear a door open
and shut. A moment later RAY's dirt-caked hand comes into
frame and gently brushes a wisp of hair back from ABBY's
face. We hear RAY walk across the apartment and a moment
later the sound of water running.*
      ABBY stirs. She looks offscreen.

LONG SHOT RAY

*Standing in the doorway to the bathroom. He is wiping his
hands on a towel.*

ABBY (*sleepily*):   . . . Ray?

RAY: You're bad.

Still half asleep, ABBY smiles.

ABBY: . . . What?

RAY: I said you're bad.

There is a long pause. Finally:

ABBY (*smiling*):   . . . You're bad too.

*RAY swings a chair out and sits down behind a table at the far
end of the room. He leans back and props his legs up on the
table. He is staring across the room at ABBY.*

RAY: We're both bad.

FADE OUT

BLACK

As we hear the click of a pull-string the camera is dropping: down past an orange safe light, down the length of its string, down to a metal darkroom tray where two short strips of negative are burning.

VISSER's hand and yellow sleeve cuff (now orange) enter frame, with an 8 × 10 black-and-white photograph. The photograph is dropped into the tray. As it burns we see that it is the same picture of ABBY's and RAY's "corpses" as VISSER showed MARTY, except that in this print the bullet holes and blood are less convincingly brushed in.

Another print is dropped into the tray and ignites. In this one we see bullet holes but no blood.

A third print is dropped in and ignites. It is the original undoctored shot of ABBY and RAY asleep in bed.

VISSER's hands enter frame holding the picture-envelope that he took away from MARTY's office. VISSER rips it in half and is about to drop it into the tray, but stops abruptly.

There is posterboard, not a photograph, peeking out of the torn envelope.

VISSER's hands pull the two halves of the placard from the envelope and fit them together. The stenciled 8 × 10 placard says: "All Employees Must Wash Hands Before Resuming Work."

LOW-ANGLE CLOSE SHOT   VISSER

Staring at the placard in disbelief.

After a moment his hand rises into frame to deposit a cigarette in his mouth. His hand drops back down, groping in a pocket.

His hand jumps back into frame, empty; he thumps at his breast pockets; he can't find his lighter.

He wheels and exits frame. The light snaps off. A door slams shut.

ABBY'S APARTMENT   DAY
CLOSE SHOT   RAY

He has dozed off in his chair. Offscreen we hear a door slam, and his eyes open.

ABBY

Emerging from the bathroom. Her voice has a flat echo in the bare apartment.

ABBY: Why didn't you get into bed?

RAY (*groggy*):   I didn't think I could sleep. I'm surprised you could. Are you all right?

ABBY: Yeah . . .

She walks over and sits down on the bed.

. . . You called me this morning.

RAY: Yeah.

ABBY looks at him, expecting more. Finally:

. . . I just wanted to let you know that everything was all right. I took care of everything. Now all we have to do is keep our heads.

ABBY: . . . What do you mean?

RAY finally looks directly at her.

RAY: I know about it, Abby. I went to the bar last night.

ABBY is looking at him in alarm.

ABBY: What happened?—Was Meurice there?

RAY: Yeah.

He laughs shortly.

. . . He didn't see me, though. Nobody saw me.

The chair grates back as he stands up and looks vaguely around the room.

. . . Is it cold in here?

ABBY *is looking at him nervously.*

ABBY: Well . . . what happened?

RAY: I cleaned it all up, but that ain't important . . .

He starts nervously pacing around the room, looking for something.

. . . What's important is what we do now; I mean we can't go around half-cocked. What we need is some time to think about this, figure it out . . .

He moves a packing crate aside, still hunting around the apartment.

. . . Anyway, we got some time now. But we gotta be smart.

ABBY: Ray—

RAY: Abby, never point a gun at anyone unless you're gonna shoot him. And when you shoot him you better make sure he's dead . . .

RAY's pacing is more agitated as he looks distractedly around the apartment.

RAY: . . . because if he's not dead he's gonna get up and try and kill you.

He pauses, seemingly at a total loss.

     . . . That's the only thing they told us in the service that was worth a goddamn—Where the hell's my windbreaker?

ABBY: What the hell happened, Ray?

RAY is walking to the window. Sunlight streams in around him.

RAY: That ain't important. What's important is that we did it. That's the only thing that matters. We both did it for each other . . .

He stoops down to look through a pile of clothes by the window.

     . . . That's what's important.

ABBY: I don't know what you're talking about.

RAY's head snaps around. Staring at her he slowly rises to his feet and then remains still.

ABBY: I . . . I mean what're you talking about, Ray? *I* haven't done anything funny.

RAY: . . . *What* was that?

ABBY, startled, can't contain her agitation anymore.

ABBY (*rapidly*):   Ray, I mean you ain't even acting like yourself. First you call me at five in the A.M. saying all kinds of nice things over the telephone and then you come charging in here scaring me half to death without even telling me what it is I'm supposed to be scared of. I gotta tell you it's extremely rattling.

RAY

We track toward him, isolating him against the window. He is perfectly still. For a long time he can't speak.

RAY (*quietly*):   . . . Don't lie to me, Abby—

BACK TO ABBY

Still worked up.

ABBY: How can I be lying if I don't even know—

The ring of the telephone cuts her off. She looks at the phone, pauses for a moment, then continues, struggling.

John Getz

. . . I mean if you and him had a fight or something, I don't care, as long as you . . .

Her voice trails off.
The telephone won't stop ringing. ABBY *and* RAY *are staring at each other, seemingly oblivious to it. Finally:*

RAY: . . . Pick it up.

CLOSE SHOT   THE TELEPHONE

Still ringing. ABBY's *hand enters frame and picks it up.*

ABBY: What.

Through the phone we hear only the rhythmic whir of a ceiling fan. ABBY *shifts the phone to her other ear, listening hard. It is the same sound we heard earlier when she picked up the phone at* RAY's *house.*
As before, the line clicks dead.

ABBY (*looking at* RAY):   . . . Welp, that was him.

There is a long moment of silence. Then RAY's *voice comes from across the room:*

RAY: . . . Who?

ABBY: Marty.

There is silence again.

LONG SHOT   THE APARTMENT

RAY *shifts in front of the window. He laughs humorlessly. The laugh stops abruptly.*

ABBY: . . . What's going on with you two?

RAY (*quietly*):   All right . . .

He starts across the room.

. . . You can call him back, whoever it was . . .

He is heading for the door.

. . . I'll get out of your way.

He pauses at the foyer and pulls ABBY's *gun out of his pocket. He sets it on a shelf by the door.*

ABBY

Watching. We hear the door open.

RAY (*os*):   You left your weapon behind.

We hear the door slam shut.

CLOSE SHOT   CEILING FAN

We hear the rhythmic whir of the fan. We tilt down from the ceiling to reveal that we are in the living room of RAY's *bungalow.*

In the foreground VISSER *sits in a chair with the cradled telephone in his lap, facing the front door, which stands open in the background. The contents of* ABBY's *tote bag lie strewn on the bureau next to* VISSER. *Her purse is not there. After a moment* VISSER *rouses himself and starts to sweep the articles back into the tote bag.*

INT   MEURICE'S APARTMENT   DAY
LOW WIDE SHOT   LIVING ROOM

It is dark, lit only by the morning light leaking in around the drawn blinds. It is a small modern apartment such as one sees in large apartment complexes—shag carpeting, built-in bar. In the extreme foreground the small red "Power" light of a telephone answering machine glows in the darkness.

The front door opens in the background, spilling bright sunlight. MEURICE stoops down, picks up two newspapers, enters, and shuts the door. He walks toward the camera and his hand enters frame in extreme foreground to punch the rewind button on the machine. His hand leaves frame. A few pieces of mail are flipped down onto the machine table, piece by piece, as the machine rewinds. He reaches down again and hits playback. After a beep:

WOMAN'S VOICE: Hi Meurice, this is Helene, Helene Trend, and I'm calling 'cause I wanna know just what the hell that remark you made about Sylvia's supposed to mean . . .

Mail continues to flip down onto the table, piece by piece.

. . . She says you're full of shit and frankly I believe her. And hey, I love you too. Sure. Anyway, you better call me soon because I'm going to South America tonight—you know, Uruguay?

Dial tone. Beep.

MARTY'S VOICE (*barking*):   Listen asshole, you know who this is. I just got back from Corpus and there's a lot of money missing from the safe . . .

The mail stops dropping; MARTY has MEURICE's attention.

. . . I'm not saying you took it but the place was your responsibility and I told you to keep an eye on your asshole friend. Don't—uh, don't come to the bar tonight, I've got a meeting. But tomorrow I want to have a word with you, and with Ray—if you can find him.

Dial tone. Beep.
   MEURICE's *hand drops into frame.*

WOMAN'S VOICE: Meurice, where the hell have you
been? I—

His finger presses the stop button.

MATCH CUT TO:
RAY'S FINGER

*Pressing into a dark stain in the upholstery of the back seat of
his car. When he raises it the fingertip is red—the seat still
wet with blood.*

CLOSE SHOT   RAY

*Looking down at the seat. He backs out of the car and walks
up the driveway to his house.*

INT   RAY'S LIVING ROOM

*As he comes through the screen door. It bangs shut behind
him. As he crosses the living room we see, and he hears,*
MEURICE's *Trans Am pulling up and stopping at the foot of
the lawn.* RAY *turns and looks out the window.*

CLOSE SHOT   CLOSET DOOR

RAY *throws it open and hurriedly pulls out the first thing at
hand—a sheet. We hear the door of the Trans Am open and
slam shut.*

EXT   RAY'S BUNGALOW
TRACKING SHOT   ON RAY

*Exiting the house as the screen door bangs and shudders
behind him. He hurries down the walk.*

TRACKING SHOT   RAY'S POV

MEURICE *is rounding the bottom of the lawn and starting up the drive toward the incriminating car. Its back door is standing ajar.*

MEURICE: I hope you're planning on leaving town.

BACK TO RAY

Reacting to the line as he reaches the car. He bends over to throw the sheet over the seat just as MEURICE *walks up behind him.*

RAY (*his back to* MEURICE; *arranging the sheet*):   Got a problem, Meurice?

MEURICE: No, you do, cowboy. You been to the bar?

RAY is still hunched in the open doorway. He freezes momentarily in arranging the sheet.

RAY: . . . Why?

MEURICE: You shouldn't have taken the money . . .

RAY doesn't reply or turn around. MEURICE *is getting more strident.*

. . . Look at me man, I'm serious. You broke in the bar and ripped off the safe . . .

RAY backs out of the car and turns around.

. . . Abby warned me you were gonna make trouble. Trouble with you is, you're too fucking obvious; the only ones with the combination are me and you . . .

RAY looks evenly at MEURICE. *Behind him the sheet has been arranged over the seat. He puts an unlit cigarette in his mouth.*

. . . and Abby. Maybe. But as far as I'm concerned that only leaves one fucking possibility.

RAY (*tonelessly*):   What's that?

MEURICE reaches out and swipes the unlit cigarette out of RAY's mouth.

MEURICE: Those things are nothing but coffin nails.

He turns and stares down the street, exasperated.

Samm-Art Williams and John Getz

. . . Look. Personally I don't give a shit. I know
Marty's a hard-on but you gotta do something. I don't
know; give the money back, say you're sorry, or get the
fuck out of here, or something . . .

*Now that his temper is gone, he realizes he has nothing much
to say. He shakes his head and turns back down the drive,
muttering as he lights himself* RAY's *cigarette.*

. . . It's very humiliating, preaching about this shit.

CLOSE SHOT   RAY

Standing in front of the back door of his car, watching
MEURICE *walk away. His right hand rises into frame to
deposit another unlit cigarette in his mouth. Offscreen,*
MEURICE *calls from the end of the drive:*

MEURICE: I'm not laughing at this, Ray Bob, so you
know it's no fucking joke.

We hear his car door slam. After a moment RAY *exits frame,
heading for the house. The camera tracks slowly in to the back
window of the car.*
     *Traces of blood are starting to seep up from the upholstery
into the sheet.*

INT   MARTY'S HOUSE   DAY
LOW WIDE SHOT   FRONT FOYER

*We are looking across the tiled floor toward the front
doorway. The room has the dim gray cast of daytime inside a
shuttered house. We hold on the empty foyer as we hear an
intermittent high whining sound. We hear the padding of feet
on carpet, and then the clatter of nails on tile as Opal,*
MARTY's *German shepherd, trots into frame and circles the
foyer, still whining. She jumps up and scratches desperately
at the front door.*
     A slow, rhythmic pounding is very faint on the track.

EXT MARTY'S BAR DUSK

ABBY *has just gotten out of her car and is walking up to the front of the darkened bar. The faint, rhythmic thumping continues over the cut, its source somewhere offscreen. As* ABBY *takes a key out of her purse and lets herself into the bar, the thumping stops.*

INT MARTY'S BAR

ABBY *switches on the lights, looks around, goes to the back-office door. Locked. As she fits her key into the lock:*

ABBY (*quietly*):   Marty?

The door swings open, fanning a shaft of light into the darkened room.

MARTY'S OFFICE BATHROOM

We are looking from the inside at the bathroom door that won't close all the way. As the light fans into the office beyond and seeps in through the crack of the bathroom door, we see VISSER's *sleeve cuff and his hand pressing against the door, to hold it near-shut.*

BACK TO ABBY

Standing in the office doorway. We pull her into the room. She stops abruptly, looking past the camera, and wrinkles her nose.

ABBY'S POV

MARTY's *fish, now half-decayed, still lie on the desk.*
     Some of the desk drawers stand open, with some of their contents strewn across the surface of the desk.

BACK TO ABBY

She takes a step forward. We hear the crunch of glass underfoot. She looks down at the floor.

ABBY'S POV

Shards of broken glass lie on the floor.

BACK TO ABBY

She looks up from the floor toward the back door.

ABBY'S POV

The pane of the back-door window closest to the knob has been shattered from the outside, scattering broken glass into the office.

BACK TO ABBY

She crosses slowly to the desk, staring at the rotted fish. She looks up from the desk.

ABBY'S POV

On the standing safe behind the desk lies a white towel. ABBY's hand enters frame and picks up the towel.
    In slow motion a hammer that's been wrapped inside slips out of the towel, falls end-over-end, hits the floor with a dull thud.

BACK TO ABBY

Stooping down to pick up the hammer. At eye level as she stoops down is the combination dial to the safe. The dial has been battered by the hammer. ABBY looks from the hammer to the floor under the desk chair.

ABBY'S POV

Blood stains.

ABBY

Staring down at the floor. She rises and looks at the desk. As she rises we hear glass under her feet.

ABBY'S POV

The dead fish. Beyond them, on the floor around the desk, broken glass.

BACK TO ABBY

Staring.

ABBY'S POV

The dead fish.

BACK TO ABBY

She seems to be falling slowly backwards. The camera falls with her, keeping her in close shot. Her head hits a pillow. We pull back slowly to reveal that she is lying on the bed in her apartment, staring across the room. She lies motionless on the bed, her eyes wide.

ABBY'S POV

Across the darkened apartment we see the curtainless windows, and beyond them, across the lamplit street, the facade of the opposite building.

LONG SHOT   ABBY

Lying still. After a moment she gets out of bed, crosses to the front door of the apartment, locks it, then walks unsteadily back to the bed.

FADE OUT

FADE IN:
SAME LONG SHOT   ABBY IN BED

She opens her eyes, lies still for a moment, coughs. She gets out of bed and walks across the still dark apartment to the bathroom. She shuts the bathroom door.

BATHROOM

ABBY *looks at herself in the mirror above the sink, then turns on the tap water. From a neighboring apartment we hear a dull rhythmic thumping on the wall. She pauses, listens for a moment, then starts to splash water on her face.*

From somewhere offscreen we hear the sharp sound of glass shattering. It reverberates for a moment, then dies. ABBY *looks up at the bathroom door. We hear a scraping at the lock of her apartment door.* ABBY *listens.*

Suddenly we hear the lock springing open, and the front door swinging on its hinges.

CLOSE SHOT   ABBY

Startled. She shuts off the water and stands motionless. Droplets of water are streaming down her face.

We hear the sound of footsteps in the next room, crunching across broken glass.

ABBY: Ray. . . ?

There is no answer. After a moment we hear bedsprings creak in the next room. ABBY *opens the bathroom door and walks out.*

MAIN ROOM

A shaft of light slices across the floor from the open bathroom door. Broken glass glints on the floor. In the semi-darkness we can see that someone is sitting on the bed. The person looks up.

It is MARTY.

ABBY *recoils.*

MARTY: Lover-boy oughta lock his door.

ABBY *looks nervously at* MARTY. *Droplets of water are still running down her face. She brushes one from her eye.*

MARTY: I love you . . .

He smiles thinly.

. . . That's a stupid thing to say, right?

ABBY takes a step back.

ABBY: I . . . I love you too.

Still smiling, MARTY shakes his head.

MARTY: No. You're just saying that because you're
scared . . .

*He stands. We hear glass under his feet. He unbuttons the
middle button of his coat and reaches inside.*

. . . You left your weapon behind.

*He withdraws something from an inside pocket and tosses it
to her.*

CLOSE SHOT   ABBY'S HANDS

As she catches the object. It is her compact.

CLOSE SHOT   ABBY

She looks from her hands up to MARTY.

MARTY: He'll kill you too.

*MARTY gags, leans forward, doubles over to vomit—blood.
The blood washes over the floor at his feet.*

ABBY

*Bolts upright in bed with a muffled groan. Sweat pours down
her face. She brushes a drop of sweat from her eye and looks
around.*

ABBY'S POV

Moonlight glints through the windows across the hardwood floor. Through the windows we can see the facade of the opposite building. The apartment is dark and still, just as we left it before she fell asleep.

BACK TO ABBY

She slumps back onto the bed. One hand gropes down out of frame and comes up holding an illuminated alarm clock. She looks at it, drops it back to the floor.

She turns on her side and stares across the room toward the window.

ABBY'S POV

The window.

DISSOLVE THROUGH TO:
SAME WINDOW   SAME ANGLE   PRE-DAWN

It is still not quite light. The few lights that shined in the windows of the opposite building before are now off; the facade of the building is a flat, undetailed gray.

CLOSE SHOT   ABBY

Still lying on her side on the bed, her eyes open, staring at the window.

BACK TO LONG SHOT   WINDOW

After a moment ABBY enters frame. She picks her coat off a chair and puts it on.

We hear a car door slam.

EXT   RAY'S BUNGALOW   PRE-DAWN

ABBY has just gotten out of her car in the foreground and is crossing the lawn to the house. Down the road the street lights are still on. One light burns in the house, in the window of RAY's bedroom. ABBY approaches it.

THROUGH THE WINDOW

Over ABBY's *shoulder, as she leans against the sill of the open window and looks inside.*

RAY *sits on the bed in the empty room, smoking a cigarette, his profile to the window, gazing fixedly at the wall.*

ABBY: Ray.

RAY *starts and looks toward the window, squinting.*

INT   RAY'S BUNGALOW
WIDE SHOT   LIVING ROOM

ABBY *is coming through the screen door. The room is strikingly bare of everything except furniture. All personal effects have been removed.*

ABBY *looks around, bewildered, as* RAY *enters from the hallway.*

ABBY: . . . Where is everything?

RAY: In the trunk.

ABBY, *still standing in front of the door, looks at him uncomprehendingly.* RAY *walks over to a couple of cardboard boxes stacked in the corner.*

. . . In the car.

He ties a knot around the top carton with a piece of cord, then cuts the cord with a collapsible fishing knife.

ABBY: . . . You leaving?

RAY: Isn't that what you want?

She slowly shakes her head.

RAY: Wanna come with me?

He leans back against the boxes, watching her.

ABBY: . . . But first I gotta know what happened.

RAY: What do you want to know?

ABBY: You broke into the bar. You wanted to get your money. You and Marty had a fight. Something happened . . .

RAY shakes his head, smiling. ABBY squints at him, looking for help.

. . . I don't know, *wasn't* it you? Maybe a burglar broke in, and you found—

RAY: With your gun? . . .

He puts the knife in his pocket and walks over to the door. As he approaches her:

. . . Nobody broke in, Abby. I'll tell you the truth . . .

RAY faces ABBY in front of the door.

RAY: . . . Truth is, I've felt sick the last couple of days. Can't eat . . . Can't sleep . . . When I try to I . . . Abby . . .

It's difficult to bring it out. RAY's hand gropes for the cross-slat on the screen door. Finally:

. . . The truth is . . . he was alive when I buried him.

ABBY *stares.*

An object materializes in the sky beyond them. It is flipping end-over-end in slow motion, moving toward ABBY *and* RAY *and the screen door.* ABBY *and* RAY, *each staring at the other, fail to notice it until—*

THWACK—*it bounces off the screen.*

ABBY *starts;* RAY *doesn't.*

The spell broken, ABBY *pushes hesitantly at the screen door.* RAY'*s hand slides off the cross-slat; he makes no move to stop her.*

CLOSE SHOT   THE FRONT STOOP

As ABBY *steps over the rolled-up newspaper that hit the screen door.*

TRACKING SHOT   ON ABBY

Hurrying down the driveway to get to her car. A low rumble is building on the soundtrack. ABBY *glances at* RAY'*s car as she passes it.*

ABBY'S POV   TRACKING FORWARD   THE CAR

More blood has seeped into and dried on the dropsheet covering the back seat. The bass rumble grows louder, punctuated by a rhythmic thumping.

EXT   MEURICE'S APARTMENT   DAY
OVER ABBY'S SHOULDER

As she pounds frantically on the door—the sound continuing over the cut. After a moment the door edges open.

MEURICE *is standing in the doorway in a long bathrobe. A sleeper's blindfold is pushed up over his forehead.*

MEURICE: Abby. What's the matter?

ABBY: I . . . I'm sorry, Meurice. I gotta talk to you . . . Can I come in?

He looks at her hard.

MEURICE: Yeah . . . yeah, come in . . .

He steps aside to let her pass.

. . . but I gotta tell ya . . .

INT   MEURICE'S APARTMENT

As ABBY enters.

MEURICE: . . . I'm retired.

MEURICE *switches on a table lamp; the curtains are drawn against the sun.* ABBY *follows* MEURICE *over to the bar.*

MEURICE: Jesus, I got a hangover. Want a drink?

ABBY: No, I—

MEURICE: Well I do . . .

He pours himself a drink.

. . . For you I answer the door. If you wanna stay here, that's fine. But I'm retired.

ABBY: Something happened with Marty and Ray—

MEURICE (*sharply*):   Abby . . .

He glares at her.

. . . Let me ask you one question . . .

He slams back his drink.

. . . Why do you think I'm retired?

He grimaces.

. . . Ray stole a shitload of money from the Marty. Until both of 'em calm down I'm not getting involved.

ABBY: No Meurice, it's worse than that. Something really happened, I think Marty's dead—

MEURICE: What?! Did Ray tell you that?

ABBY: Sort of . . .

MEURICE sits her down on the sofa.

MEURICE: That's total bullshit. Marty called me *after* he was jacked up . . .

He tries to coax her into lying down.

. . . I mean, I don't know where he is, but he ain't dead.

ABBY: Meurice—

MEURICE: You don't look too good. You sleep last night?

Her head meets an end cushion.

ABBY: Meurice, you gotta help me . . .

MEURICE rises from the sofa, sighs.

MEURICE: All right. Just sit tight. Try to get some sleep . . .

He leans down to the table next to the sofa.

. . . I'll find Marty, find out what's going on.

CLOSE SHOT　ABBY

Her head on the cushion. We hear engine rumble. ABBY *twists her head back, following* MEURICE. *As we hear the table lamp being switched off we:*

CUT TO:
EXT　HIGHWAY　NIGHT
POV FROM A CAR

The engine rumble continues over the cut. There is no other traffic on the highway. A light fog covers the road. A green highway sign says: "San Antonio 73 mi." We hear a car radio playing softly.

CLOSE SHOT　RAY

Driving. He is gently lit by the light from the dashboard. He reaches forward to turn off the radio. The only sound now is the hum of the engine and the rhythmic clomping of tires on pavement. The look and sound of the scene are close to those of the first scene of the movie.

　　RAY *takes a cigarette out of his pocket and puts it in his mouth, but leaves it unlit.*

RAY'S POV

The headlights of an approaching car materialize in the fog. The car passes with a roar.

　　Up ahead a traffic light is just turning amber.

BACK TO RAY

The engine hum drops as he slows. We hear the low engine rumble and the squeaking brakes of another car. RAY *is now stopped in front of the deserted intersection. He looks up in his rearview mirror.*

RAY'S POV

Another car is stopped just behind him, the fog floating up past its headlights. The headlights halate in the fog; none of the rest of the car is visible.

BACK TO RAY

The unlit cigarette still in his mouth. He looks down from the rearview mirror to the intersection ahead of him. There is a long pause, during which we hear only the steady purr of RAY's car and the knocking rumble of the car behind him.
RAY looks up at the traffic light.

RAY'S POV

The light is just turning from red to green.

CLOSE SHOT   RAY'S FOOT ON BRAKE

He takes his foot off the brake, hesitates for a moment, then replaces it on the brake.

CLOSE SHOT   RAY

He looks up in his rearview mirror.

RAY'S POV

The headlights of the other car remain motionless behind him. The car makes no move to pass.

BACK TO RAY

He slowly takes the cigarette from his mouth and drops it onto the seat next to him. His eyes shift from the rearview mirror to the traffic light.

RAY'S POV

Green fog floats up past the green light.

BACK TO RAY

His face frozen. He turns slowly to look behind.

RAY'S POV

The other car is still motionless. We hear the muted rumble of its engine.

BACK TO RAY

His eyes shift back to the mirror. He gropes for his window handle and slowly rolls it down. He sticks out his left arm, eyes still on the rearview mirror, and waves for the other car to go around him.

RAY'S POV

The other car remains still for a moment. White fog floats up beyond the red fog created by RAY's *brake lights.*
Finally the car pulls out slowly to the left to pass.

BACK TO RAY

Watching the car pass.

RAY'S POV

As the car pulls out into the light from the intersection and RAY's *headlights, we see that it is a battered green Volkswagen. First the car itself, and then its red tail lights, disappear into the fog.*

BACK TO RAY

Watching, for a long moment.
Finally he takes his foot off the brake, turns the steering wheel hard left and hangs a U-turn.

MARTY'S LIVING ROOM   WIDE

A light is switched on in the expensively appointed room.
MEURICE *enters, walking silently on the carpet, looking*

around the room. He throws the light off at the far end and leaves.

MARTY'S BEDROOM WIDE

The door swings open. MEURICE *throws the switch near the door and the room is bathed in light. We are once again in the bedroom where we earlier saw* ABBY *looking through her purses.*
We start to hear the faint buzzing of a fly.
MEURICE *glances around, throws off the light, and shuts the door. Black.*

MARTY'S OFFICE

Somewhere offscreen a light is switched on and we are looking in close shot at the dead fish.
The sound of the fly is louder with the cut.

CLOSE SHOT RAY

Standing in the doorway from the bar, staring down at the fish.

WIDE SHOT THE OFFICE

RAY *glances around at the broken glass lying on the floor. His gaze shifts to the safe and the hammer in front of it. He walks over to the safe and stoops down.*

CLOSE SHOT RAY AT SAFE

He works its battered dial and it swings open. He shuffles through the contents and brings out a small pile of photographs.

RAY'S POV

As he flips through the photographs. The first four are RAY *and* ABBY *in the motel room bed. The last is a mounted 8 × 10:* ABBY *and* MARTY *on a Gulf beach.*

BACK TO RAY

Looking.

HIS POV   PICTURE DETAIL

MARTY *is still laughing.*

BACK TO RAY

He scowls at the shots VISSER *took, then puts them back in the safe. When his hand comes out he is holding another photograph—this one folded twice. He unfolds it.*

RAY'S POV

His and ABBY's *corpses.*

BACK TO RAY   FROM ACROSS THE DESK

As he straightens slowly from the safe in the background.
   At desk level, we again see the glint of VISSER's *lighter under the dead fish.*
   RAY *crosses slowly around the desk into the foreground and lays the picture flat on the desktop. For a moment he stares down at it, then wheels abruptly and leaves frame.*

INT   RAY'S CAR
CLOSE SHOT   RAY

Driving. He glances up in the rearview mirror.

MARTY'S KITCHEN

As MEURICE *enters and throws an overhead light. The white room is bathed in bright, shadowless light. As* MEURICE *steps into the kitchen his foot strikes something on the floor below frame, which clatters hollowly away.*

CLOSE SHOT   PLASTIC DOG-FOOD BOWL

The empty bowl skids into a wall, bounces back, and wobbles, spinning on its bottom rim.

MARTY'S BILLIARD ROOM
DUTCH-TILT
TRACKING SHOT   TOWARD MOUNTED MOOSE HEAD

*On a low skewed axis the camera is tracking in toward the
impassive trophy head on* MARTY's *billiard-room wall.*
   The moose still has RAY's *cigarette protruding from its
mouth.*

REVERSE TRACKING SHOT   MEURICE

*As he walks toward the moose, head cocked to one side,
frowning quizzically up.*
   He hears something, and looks through the door to his left.

MEURICE'S POV

The long shadowy hall. We hear panting.

CLOSE SHOT   MEURICE

Squinting.

MEURICE: . . . Opal?

THE HALLWAY

A form starts to materialize in the shadows.

MEURICE

Taking a step back.

HIS POV

*The dog bounding down the hallway. Its panting has become
a low growl.*

FROM BEHIND MEURICE

He wrenches a cue stick from the rack and squares.

HIS POV

Opal snarling, leaping.

INT MEURICE'S APARTMENT
CLOSE SHOT TOP OF A COFFEE TABLE

The splintered top half of the pool cue is slammed down to rest on top of the coffee table.

MEURICE (*os*):   Even the fucking dog's gone crazy . . .

MED SHOT ABBY

Sitting on the sofa, looking down out of frame. Behind her MEURICE *agitatedly paces back and forth, waving the splintered bottom half of the cue stick. His voice is unnaturally loud.*

MEURICE: . . . Something pretty fucking weird is going on. Put your coat on and I'll drop you at home. But don't talk to either of 'em until I do. And don't worry. Believe me. These things always have a logical explanation. Usually.

ABBY'S POV

The splintered top half of the cue stick on the coffee table.

INT ABBY'S HALLWAY

ABBY *approaches her door in the foreground and lets herself in.*

INT ABBY'S APARTMENT

Looking toward the window. The room is dark. Through the window we see the facade of the building across the street. ABBY *enters frame in the foreground, in silhouette against the window, and throws an overhead light switch. The bright light reveals* RAY *standing by the window, looking out.*

RAY (*abruptly*):   Turn it off.

ABBY *jumps, startled.*

ABBY: Ray . . .

EXT   ROOF OF FACING APARTMENT BUILDING

From the roof of the building across the street we are looking down on the facade of ABBY's building. Most of its windows are dark, but in a brightly lit fourth-floor window we can clearly see ABBY and RAY.

A man is on the roof in the foreground, hitching a rifle to his shoulder.

INT   ABBY'S APARTMENT

RAY turns from the window which, with the switching on of the overhead light, has become a mirror of the interior of the apartment.

RAY: Just turn it off.

EXT   FACING ROOF

The light goes out in the apartment across the street; its window goes opaque.

INT   ABBY'S APARTMENT

Dark now. RAY still stands by the window, looking out. ABBY still stands by the light switch.

RAY (*answering a question*): No curtains on the windows.

ABBY is clearly apprehensive—about RAY, not about anything outside.

ABBY: . . . So?

RAY: I think someone's watching.

ABBY doesn't understand, and has had enough. As she throws the light back on:

ABBY: So what'll they see?

RAY turns angrily from the window.

RAY: Just leave it off. He can see in.

EXT FACING ROOF

RAY and ABBY are once again clearly visible. RAY is starting across the room.

INT ABBY'S APARTMENT

ABBY takes a fearful step back as RAY strides toward the light switch, next to her.

ABBY (*abruptly*):   —If you do anything the neighbors'll hear.

This brings RAY up short. He stares at ABBY. It registers that it is him she's afraid of.

RAY: You think . . .

He shakes his head.

. . . Abby. I meant it . . . when I called . . .

ABBY takes another step back. Her voice comes out, after a pause, half-strangled:

ABBY: . . . I love you too.

RAY winces. He slowly shakes his head with a pained half-smile.

RAY: Because you're scared.

We hear the dull report of a rifle and the deafening sound of shattering glass. The gun shot hits RAY in the back, knocking him to the floor. He lies still.

CLOSE SHOT   ABBY

She stares dumbly down at RAY. She looks slowly up to the window.

THE WINDOW

It has a gaping black hole. The sound of shattering glass still reverberates in the apartment. Small shards of glass chink down from the window and shatter on the floor.

BACK TO ABBY

Staring at the window, paralyzed—almost in a trance. Quiet except for the chinking of glass.

EXT   FACING ROOF

We are looking through the telescopic sight of a high-powered rifle. The rifle sweeps up from RAY's body across the brightly lit room, and centers ABBY, still staring at the window, in the cross hairs.

INT   ABBY'S APARTMENT

We are looking past ABBY toward the shattered window at the far end of the room. A brass lamp stands in the foreground, between ABBY and the camera. ABBY still stands paralyzed.

Glass has stopped chinking from the window to the floor; there is a painful silence.

Suddenly ABBY dives to the floor just as CRASH the rest of the window falls away and PING the brass lamp somersaults toward us from the impact of the bullet.

The window is now completely gone—just a black hole in the brightly lit wall.

ABBY

Scrambles into a corner at the window end of the room. The only sound is her heavy breathing. She looks over at RAY, *then up at the bulb on the ceiling.*

ABBY'S POV   CEILING BULB

BACK TO ABBY

Breathing heavily, almost hysterical. She looks down at the floor.

ABBY'S POV

RAY *is sprawled on the floor in a pool of blood and broken glass.*

BACK TO ABBY

She reaches down and pulls off one of her shoes. She throws it at the ceiling bulb.
  We hear the bulb shatter and the room goes black.
  ABBY *rises and makes her way cautiously across the glass-littered floor toward* RAY. *She stoops over him.*

LOW SHOT   THE DARK APARTMENT

Its front door in the background. ABBY *rises into frame and backs toward the doorway, staring down at the floor. One of her hands is covered with blood.*

ABBY: Ray—

She winces and almost loses her balance as we hear a piece of glass crunching under her bare foot. She turns and moves to the front door, favoring one foot, and throws the door open.

HALLWAY

ABBY *lurches from her apartment and pounds on the neighboring door. No answer. She pounds on the door across the hall.*

OLD WOMAN'S VOICE (*frightened, in Spanish*):   Get away!
I'll call my son-in-law!

ABBY (*groping for the words, in Spanish*):   No no—you
don't understand—

OLD WOMAN'S VOICE (*in Spanish*):   He has a gun!

> *ABBY heads for the stairway at the far end of the hall. The heel
> of her shod foot is throwing her weight onto her bad foot; she
> kicks off the shoe.*

CLOSE SHOT   ABBY

*As she reaches the top of the stairs. She takes one step down,
then brings herself up short. She looks over the railing down
the stairwell. It is quiet. An innocent-sounding cough echoes
somewhere in the building.*

> *We hear the sound of footsteps from somewhere below.*
> *ABBY turns and hobbles back to her apartment. The
> bareness of the hallway sets off her abandoned shoe.*

ABBY'S APARTMENT

*As she enters and slams the door behind her. She scrabbles at
the lock, finally manages to get it shut, then turns and looks
frantically around.*

ABBY'S POV

RAY is lying still in the darkness.

> *We can hear footsteps approaching up the hallway.*
> *ABBY enters frame and kneels down next to RAY. She
> fumbles around him briefly in the darkness.*
> *The doorknob rattles. ABBY freezes, listening, trying to
> control her breath. After a moment we hear a scraping at the
> lock.*
> *ABBY moves to the bathroom adjoining the main room and
> shuts the door behind her.*

BATHROOM

It is very small. ABBY *presses her palms against the door and slowly eases her ear against the door to listen. The scraping in the apartment door lock continues. Sweat streams down* ABBY's *face. She brushes a drop from her eye.*

We hear the snap of the lock springing open, and the front door swinging on its hinges.

CLOSER ON ABBY

Her ear pressed to the door. From the next room we hear the sound of footsteps crunching across broken glass.

ABBY *backs away from the door, stares at it, then turns and moves to the bathroom window. She looks out.*

ABBY'S POV

A sheer drop to the narrow backyard of the building four stories below. Next to ABBY's *window is another window, separated from hers only by the breadth of the wall, that separates the two apartments.*

ABBY'S APARTMENT

VISSER *hunches, hands on knees, over* RAY, *who lies on the floor out of frame.*

VISSER (*grimly*):   All right . . .

He hunkers down closer to RAY.

. . . You got some of my personal property.

He is rummaging through RAY's *pockets but comes up empty-handed.*

. . . One of you does.

VISSER *looks down at* RAY, *glances around the room, looks back down at* RAY.

. . . I don't know what the hell you two thought you were gonna pull.

His hand, gripping something, flashes down out of frame. We hear a dull crunch.

BATHROOM

ABBY *has drawn her head back from the bathroom window. She moves back to the door and braces herself against it.*

ABBY'S APARTMENT

VISSER *straightens up from* RAY's *body. He drops something to the floor, out of frame, that lands with a thud.*
    He goes over to the light switch on the wall and flips it back and forth. No light.
    He goes over to the brass lamp, sets it upright, tries its switch. Again nothing.
    He disappears into the kitchenette as we hold on its open doorway. After a moment we hear a refrigerator hum as a cold blue light plays on the doorway. There is the rattle of a can being pulled off the refrigerator rack, and the snap of its pull-tab being opened. After a couple of audible slurps we hear the can go back on the rack and, as the blue light disappears, we hear the refrigerator door close.
    VISSER *reappears in the doorway. He surveys the room, fixes on the bathroom door, goes over, turns the knob. The door swings open.*
    He walks in.

BATHROOM

VISSER *looks around the cramped space. The shower curtain is drawn. He casually draws it back. The shower is empty.*
    He goes to the window and leans out.

VISSER'S POV

The sheer drop below; the other window to one side.

BACK TO VISSER

*He draws his head back in, presses his palms against the
adjacent wall, and eases his ear to the wall to listen.*
  Perfect quiet.
  *After a moment he goes back to the window, braces himself
against the sash, and sticks his arm out—groping for the
window of the adjacent apartment.*

EXT   ABBY'S BUILDING/BATHROOM WINDOW
CLOSE SHOT   VISSER'S FACE

*Pressing against the glass as he leans against the upper half
of the bathroom window.*

CLOSE SHOT   VISSER'S HAND

It finds the adjacent window and starts to raise it.

BACK TO VISSER'S FACE

*Again we see him through the window. His jaw is set as he
gropes offscreen.*
  *Suddenly his body jerks violently forward, his head
smacking against the glass and cracking it.*

QUICK CUT TO:
INT   ADJACENT APARTMENT
CLOSE SHOT   VISSER'S HAND

ABBY *(out of frame) has grabbed it and now THUMP she
slams the window down on his wrist, catching it between the
window sash and sill.*
  Her other hand flashes across frame to THUNK pin
VISSER's *hand to the sill with* RAY's *knife.*

QUICK CUT:
BACK TO VISSER

*We hear the shatter of glass as the shock causes his head to
break through the window. His hand is nailed into the
apartment next door. He is in pain.*

ADJACENT APARTMENT

ABBY *backs slowly from the window, staring at the hand.*
From the ground below we hear the faint and echoing sounds
of the shards of glass shattering against pavement.

ABBY'S POV THE WINDOW

VISSER's *pinned hand is writhing.*
    As we hear a muffled CRACK, a circle of light opens with
a puff of plaster dust in the wall that separates the two
apartments. A line of light shoots across the dark apartment
from the bright bathroom next door.

BACK TO ABBY

Staring at the wall. We hear a second CRACK.

ABBY'S POV

A second small hole has opened in the wall, letting through a
second shaft of light.
    Four more sharp reports in rapid succession: With each
gun blast a bright circle opens and a new shaft of light
penetrates the dark apartment.
    Finally we hear the CLICK of an empty chamber, and the
clatter of the empty gun being dropped to the floor of the
bathroom next door.

CLOSE SHOT ABBY

Staring at the lines of light that crisscross the apartment.
    There is a long moment of silence, then a sudden THUMP.

ABBY'S POV THE WALL

Six circles of light.
    The circles go black momentarily as there is another
THUMP. And another. Each time VISSER *pounds his fist*
against the wall, there is a muffled THUMP and his
swinging arm strobes the bullet holes.

M. Emmet Walsh

BACK TO ABBY

She turns and hobbles toward the door of the apartment. The muffled thumping continues, as in her dream.

HALLWAY

As ABBY emerges from the adjacent apartment. She stops and looks down the hall.

ABBY'S POV

The stairway is at the far end of the hall. The door of her own darkened apartment stands slightly ajar.

ADJACENT APARTMENT
CLOSE SHOT   THE WALL

The bullet holes strobing. The pounding, more purposeful now, grows louder and more intense.

Finally, with a crash, VISSER's fist penetrates the wall in an explosion of light and dust.

HALLWAY

We pull ABBY *as she limps hesitantly down the hall.*

ADJACENT APARTMENT
CLOSE SHOT   VISSER'S HAND

*Waving aimlessly through the ambient dust. He is blindly
groping for the sill—and the knife that pins his other hand.*
  *His outstretched middle finger just grazes the handle of the
knife.*

ABBY'S HALLWAY/APARTMENT

Pulling ABBY *as she draws even with the door of her
apartment.*

ABBY'S POV

*Her pearl-handled revolver sits on the shelf just inside the
door, where* RAY *left it. It catches the light from the hall.*

ADJACENT APARTMENT
EXTREME CLOSE SHOT   VISSER'S FINGERTIPS

*The side of his middle finger rubs against the knife handle; the
tip of his index finger barely touches it.* VISSER's *fingers are
trembling, indicating that his arm is stretched to its
uttermost.*
  *A surge against the wall gives his fingers another inch or
so and they curl around the handle of the knife.*

ABBY'S APARTMENT
CLOSE SHOT   ABBY

*As she steps in from the hallway to pick up the gun. She looks
around the apartment.*

ABBY'S POV

*The window of the apartment, its glass now completely gone,
lets in streetlight.* RAY's *corpse is a dark form in the middle of*

the floor. A bright shaft of light slices across the room from offscreen. It glints on the shards of glass that litter the floor, just as in ABBY's dream.

BATHROOM
CLOSE SHOT   VISSER

As he slowly, quietly draws his hand in from the hole in the wall. He is holding the knife.
  He turns slowly to face the door, listening.

ABBY'S APARTMENT
CLOSE SHOT   ABBY

She steadies herself against the wall and turns to look toward the bathroom.

ABBY'S POV

The bathroom door stands slightly ajar. The interior of bathroom is a bright band in the shadowy recesses of the back of the apartment.

BATHROOM
CLOSE SHOT   VISSER

Moving quietly toward the door.

ABBY'S APARTMENT
CLOSE SHOT   ABBY

Staring, almost transfixed, at the bathroom door. She raises the gun, trembling, and trains it on the band of light.

ABBY'S POV

VISSER's shadow falls across the crack in the doorway.

BACK TO ABBY

She shifts the gun slightly and fires.

Frances McDormand

ABBY'S POV

With the roar of the gun, a small circle of light opens in the door. As the door waffles under the impact, we hear VISSER *collapsing behind it.*

BACK TO ABBY

Leaning against the facing wall. She lowers the gun. She slides down the wall to finally rest seated on the floor. She brushes a drop of sweat from her eye.

HER POV

The cracked bathroom door spilling light.

BACK TO ABBY

A pause. After a moment, her voice comes out half-choked:

ABBY: . . . I ain't afraid of you, Marty.

HER POV

The bathroom door. Quiet for a long moment.
   Then, from inside the bathroom, we hear laughter.

BACK TO ABBY

Staring at the door. We hear the laughter subside, to leave the sound of labored breathing. Finally:

VISSER (*os*):   . . . Well ma'am . . .

BATHROOM

VISSER *lies on his back, his head underneath the bathroom sink.*
   His good hand is pressed against his belly, which rises and falls with his heavy breathing. Blood seeps out between his fingers.
   He is smiling.

VISSER: . . . If I see him, I'll sure give him the message.

HIS POV

The underside of the sink, its convoluted chrome works beading moisture.

VISSER

Looking, with mild interest.

HIS POV

A condensed droplet trickles down the chrome.
Directly overhead, it hangs for a moment from the lowest joint of the pipe.
It fattens, wavers, wavers—and falls, spelling . . .

FINIS